"*Reworship* is a needed wake-up call. Mike challenges the church to move beyond momentary worship and return to a life fully oriented around God. This book isn't about hype—this is a call to become true worshipers and steward a new move of God. Clear, prophetic, and deeply pastoral, *Reworship* invites disciples back to renew their reverence to God, and that is where true transformation begins."

Joseph Pringle, *Pastor of C3OC Church*

"Before becoming a missions leader, I was a worship leader. But worship is still at the heart of what I do in missions work. Mike Seay gets to that convergence and to a realization that I and so many others have experienced: Worship moves us beyond the Sunday routines. *Reworship* is a soul-stirring call to make worshiping Jesus the heartbeat of everyday life. With biblical insight, pastoral warmth, and clear practical guidance, Mike traces our deep restlessness back to Eden and shows how wholehearted worship realigns our peace, purpose, relationships, and mission. I highly recommend this book if you're a worship leader looking to move people beyond Sunday mornings. But I also recommend it to a mission leader looking to connect your people in deeper worship of Jesus and the Father."

Daniel Yang, *Senior Director of Global Missions and Church Movements, World Relief*

"Mike writes with warmth, deep pastoral insight, and beautiful conviction. *Reworship* isn't merely a book; it's a refreshing invitation to rediscover the beauty of worship in our everyday lives. I've been personally blessed by Mike's wisdom and friendship over the years, and I know you will be too."

Nick Connolly, *Pastor, Bright City Church, Author of* Don't Give Up Just Yet *and* Bible Promises for Dads

"*Reworship* calls us back to the essence of worship—not performance, not routine, but a surrendered life centered on God. With clarity and depth, Mike Seay invites readers to rediscover longing, reimagine worship's meaning, and recommit to a daily life of worship that transforms both heart and community. This is a timely and needed read for anyone longing to worship with renewed sincerity and purpose."

Deborah Hong , *Worship Leader, Songwriter, North Palm Worship*

"I've known Mike for many years, and one thing always shines through—his passion for God's glory. Like Moses, this book *Reworship* calls us to take off our shoes and cry, "If Your presence doesn't go with us, do not send us." This book will help you and the people around you to gaze on the glory of God in the face of Jesus. Let *Reworship* reorient you to become the worshipers Jesus spoke of—the worshipers the Father seeks."

Peyton Jones, *Author of* Discipology *and* Church Plantology

*re*worship

HOW TO RETURN TO TRUE WORSHIP, AND WHY THAT CHANGES EVERYTHING

MIKE SEAY

This book is dedicated to Carolina Forest Community Church. Although it is a church, it represents so much more to me.

It was the place where God first revealed Himself to me and where He would continue to reveal Himself in powerful ways.

It's where I chose to believe in and began to follow Jesus.

It's where I started learning music.

It's where my deepest friendships were formed.

It's where I first saw the most beautiful woman walk through its front doors—the woman who would become my wife.

It was a place where I was given opportunities to grow, the grace to get things wrong, and eventually the responsibility to lead. So much of what lives inside this book was shaped there by learning to listen to what God was doing and practicing following Him.

More than any other place, this was where I first explored the presence of God through music.

This place was soil. And so much of me grew there—my relationship with God, my calling, and my understanding of worship.

So thank you for being a place where God met me and shaped me, and for giving me room to become who He was calling me to be.

CONTENTS

My favorite authors and communicators have a way of taking deeply complex truths and making them beautifully simple. That's exactly what Mike has done with *Reworship*. Like a brand-new hymn, it feels fresh yet timeless. Each chapter reads like a familiar friend—warm, honest, and full of revelation.

Mike and I have been best friends since we were nine years old. From running the halls of the church my parents planted to learning guitar in our middle school praise band, to worship college and beyond, I've had a front-row seat to his life. I am proud to say I've watched him pursue a life of worship and work to live out every word of this book.

There are several reasons I'm grateful you're holding this book in your hands.

Over the years, I've had the opportunity to travel and witness people worship God all over the world. There is something unforgettable about watching people praise without restraint— voices lifted, hands raised, hearts fully engaged. But there is something even more powerful than that. There are moments when you can step into a room and instantly sense that what's happening didn't start there. The worship isn't manufactured. It's overflow. It's the sound of people who have been loving and pursuing God all week.

That's the kind of worship this book calls us back to.

As a worship leader in the local church for most of my life, I've led in rooms that felt alive and rooms that felt heavy. I've seen what happens when praise becomes performance, and I've experienced what happens when praise flows from pursuing God's presence. This book doesn't just talk about music. It pulls us beyond sound and back to the heart—back to the daily pursuit of God that makes our musical worship an overflow.

A few years ago, at a time when it felt like I was living out some of my biggest prayers—writing music with heroes of mine, watching doors open I never imagined, encountering God in powerful ways—I found myself in a place I had never been before. In the middle of all that visible "success," I was battling depression for the first time in my life.

One of the things that grounded me and transformed me the most in that season was a simple piece of wisdom a counselor shared with me: "Go to God first and most."

That encouragement reshaped my rhythms. It wasn't about trying harder or doing more. It was about order. It was about learning to be satisfied in God and resting in how fully satisfied He is with me, not because of anything I could accomplish but simply because I am His son.

I believe this book helps each of us return to that place— where we see ourselves rightly, where intimacy comes before activity, and where our deepest satisfaction is found in Christ.

It almost feels limiting to call this a book. It's more like an invitation—an invitation back to the very thing we were created for. *Reworship* reminds us that it's not complicated.

As you turn these pages, read slowly. Let them realign you. Let them call you back to your first love. My prayer is that this book won't simply reshape how you think about worship but that it will restore the way you live it.

Brandon Lake

If you get worship right, you will get everything else right.

I f I asked you to picture worship, you would probably imagine a church sanctuary, a worship leader, a band or choir, a congregation singing, and, depending on the church, maybe people raising their hands.

This isn't wrong. This picture is worship, but it barely scratches the surface of what worship was meant to be. Most of us never intended to restrict worship, but little by little, the routines and experiences of life have shrunk our understanding of what is available to us. Somewhere along the way, we've put worship in a box—limited what it means, how it happens, and what it looks like.

We have settled for far less than we were made for. When we cram worship into activities and rituals, we shrink our experience down to passing moments and Sunday services, never realizing we're limiting the full life God has designed for us.

This is why so many believers feel restless, unsatisfied, or unfulfilled—even while genuinely trying to seek God.

When we narrow our understanding and practice of worship, the life-changing wholeness God offers stays just out of reach. We anxiously press through busy days, hoping we don't miss anything important, and end up wondering whether we're doing enough or doing things right. We search for the "peace of God, which transcends all understanding" that we read about in Philippians 4:7, but it still seems distant, no matter how hard we try. How can we reach the end of the day with more peace, more joy, and more fulfillment?

It all starts with worship. Everything comes back to worship.

I'm convinced that when you get worship right, you will get everything else right.

If you can open your mind to a broader understanding of what worship is, why we do it, and how we do it, you can unleash the power to transform every part of your life —your work, relationships, and quiet moments—into divine connection with God. It's time to step back from our preconceived ideas about worship.

A former pastor of mine once said, "Worship is what has your heart's affection and your mind's attention." I love the simplicity of that statement because it reframes worship not as an event or ritual but as the deep orientation of our whole being toward God. When our heart's affection and mind's attention are centered on His will and glory, every part of our lives begins to realign.

Eventually, our actions, hopes, and values reflect the shape of God's purpose, and we find ourselves moving toward the fulfillment and peace that seemed so elusive before.

With worship at the foundation, we don't just survive. We thrive.

Worshiping God doesn't end at the sanctuary door. It follows us into every environment, bringing clarity and intentionality to every part of our lives. When worshiping God becomes the main aim of your life, it starts to affect everything—how you handle doubts, how quickly you forgive, and how deeply at home you feel with God and His people (Colossians 3:17).

With this book, I want to help you move worship out of a narrow box that many have unintentionally put it in. I want to help free you from empty practices and performative actions that maintain the distance you might feel from God. I want to remove limitations and guide you in embracing the full, expansive, and compelling life as God intends, by way of worshiping Him.

It's time for believers to renew their intimacy with God and refresh their lives with true worship. It's time to reworship. This renewal isn't just for a select few. It's for every believer who longs for all God has for them—deeper meaning, greater purpose, and life to the full (John 10:10).

REVIVAL, REFORMATION, AND REWORSHIP

It's exciting when a revival breaks out. History is full of moments when God moved so powerfully that He shook entire communities awake.

I think of times like these:

> The First Great Awakening of the 1730s and 1740s when the Holy Spirit stirred spiritual hunger across the American colonies and England, and preachers like Jonathan Edwards, George Whitefield, and John Wesley simply joined in what God was already doing.

- The Welsh Revival of 1904–1905 where an estimated 100,000 people came to Christ through simple, Spirit-led gatherings of worship, prayer, repentance, and song—not because of a celebrity leader but through a praying people.

- The Azusa Street Revival (1906–1915) where a small, humble community in Los Angeles, led in part by William Seymour, became a catalyst for modern Pentecostalism as the Spirit was poured out on ordinary men and women.

- The Jesus Movement of the 1960s and 1970s when thousands of young adults in the counterculture encountered Jesus, and the sound and culture of worship were reshaped in living rooms, beaches, and simple church gatherings.

I love these moments. I honor them.

Revivals and reformations are gifts. They are signposts of God's mercy in moments when people return to Him with urgency and hunger.

But here is the part we often don't consider: Revival, by nature, is a *response* to a moment—a moment of God's divine movement. Revivals are powerful, but they surge to life in certain places and seasons, and then they come to a close. Revivals end.

You might be ready to argue, "But Mike, if I carry the spirit of revival with me in my heart, then I'm keeping the revival alive." I think it's amazing when we can keep the spirit of revival alive inside us. In fact, it's imperative. But I would argue that once you cross over into carrying the spirit of revival with you wherever you go, it's not revival anymore. You've transitioned into living a life of worship—and that brings us to the heart of this book.

The invitation to reworship is not limited to a place or a moment. It's a call to renewed intimacy with God, wherever you are and as long as you live. It's a call to enjoy each day refreshed by worship that goes far beyond the Sunday service. It's reconnecting with our true purpose—to worship God and reflect Him in every part of our lives.

Reworship asks a different question: What if the way we lean into God during revival became the way we live with Him every day?

If we desired to walk with God first—above everything else—we wouldn't need to chase revival or wait for reformation. We would be living in the very intimacy those movements point us toward. That's easier said than done, yes. But it is possible. And it's the heartbeat of this book.

Reworship is meant to shape a lifetime, not just a moment. It's an invitation to enjoy each day refreshed by worship that goes far beyond the Sunday service.

AN INVITATION TO REWORSHIP

We are not the first people to drift from God's design for worship, turning it into something less than He intended.

Take King Josiah. In 2 Kings 22, the once-united kingdom had split. The northern kingdom of Israel had already fallen, and many of Judah's kings had turned their backs on God.

In the midst of this spiritual decline, Josiah's priests discovered the forgotten Book of the Law during Temple repairs. Josiah read its words, and he was heartbroken. He realized how far God's people had wandered, and he called everyone to turn back, renew their covenant, remove idols, and worship God with new devotion.

History repeated itself about two centuries later. Judah had fallen, and the people of God had been exiled in foreign lands for seventy years. Away from home, surrounded by other cultures and pressures, many lost their focus and compromised their worship again.

But God made a way back. When they returned to Jerusalem, leaders such as Zerubbabel rebuilt the Temple, and Ezra found the same Book of the Law. He read it aloud and invited the people to respond.

As they listened, something awakened. They stood for hours, wept, raised their hands, and bowed in humility. And in that response—sparked not by finding a book but by hearing God's heart—they worshiped again. It was a return to the very reason they were created: to worship God in truth and with their whole hearts.

TIMELINE OF WORSHIP

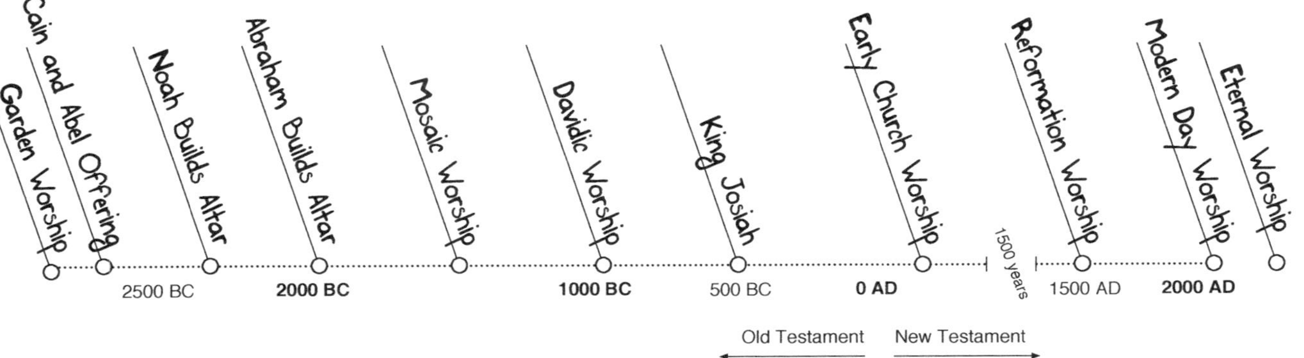

To learn more: Scan the QR code or
visit reworship.com/timeline.

Why does this matter for us? Josiah and Ezra remind us that every generation drifts and that every generation can rediscover true worship. Their stories show how God meets us in our return and how renewal always starts with honest recognition of where we've settled for less.

You may not have crafted a golden statue to worship. On the contrary, you might go to church every Sunday, tithe, volunteer, and listen to praise music in your car. But even with all these good habits, many of us are still missing out on the fullness God intended for us.

According to Romans 12:1, real worship isn't just about rituals or routines. It's offering our whole lives to God, letting every part of who we are become an act of devotion. This kind of worship unlocks the deeper relationship and purpose we're made for.

Today, we have the same opportunity to rediscover the relationship God intended and let it shape every way we worship Him. It's time for us—no matter where we find ourselves in life—to rediscover worship for what it truly is, and to give it all to God.

This book is not just an invitation. It's a challenge to break free from habits and beliefs that have diminished your understanding of worship. I encourage you to open your heart and allow God to refresh, expand, and deepen your worship far beyond the walls of the church and into the heart of every moment.

Will you join me on this journey? Together, we'll explore:

What worship looks like
How we worship
Where we worship
Why we worship
Who can worship

Let's embrace the fullness of worship and rediscover the peace, joy, and purpose we were created for.

As you read on, I invite you to set aside any assumptions or routines that have shaped your understanding of worship. The chapters ahead will explore why worship is woven into our very purpose, how it heals our broken places, and what it truly means to live in daily connection with God.

If you've ever felt a longing for something deeper, you're in the right place.

Let's begin this journey by rediscovering the original design for worship and uncovering the joy, peace, and fulfillment it brings.

You are worthy, our Lord and
God, to receive glory and honor
and power, for you created all
things, and by your will they were
created and have their being.

REVELATION 4:11

REDISCOVER: THE LONGING – WHY YOU WERE MADE

magine this. It's Sunday morning, and your family is trying to get to church on time. The kitchen smells like burned toast. Someone's still hunting for missing shoes, and voices are getting louder and sharper. The clock keeps ticking, and patience starts wearing thin. In the middle of the chaos, you can't find the car keys while someone else frantically searches for the spare that is buried in the junk drawer.

Finally, everyone piles into the car for the drive that should, in theory, be peaceful—but instead, it feels more like a silent truce. You say to yourself, "We shouldn't fight on the way to church." There are a few deep breaths, a few forced smiles, maybe even a muttered apology as you pull into the church parking lot. You straighten your clothes, try to adjust your attitude, and walk through those doors, all while carrying the weight of the morning on your shoulders.

And then the music begins. The lights dim. People around you lift their hands and start to sing. But inside, you're still catching your breath, still trying to recover from the whirlwind that just happened, but you're supposed to worship now. You're supposed to focus your heart, quiet your mind, and offer something sacred.

In that moment, you can't help but ask honest, lingering questions: *Why does this feel so hard? What are we going through all of this trouble for?*

Maybe your morning wasn't as frantic as this scenario. Maybe you arrived calmly and peacefully, but as the service began, you still wondered why you have to spend the first half of it doing something you don't connect with. Why don't you feel like everyone else seems to during the worship service? Why aren't the songs impacting you the way they're impacting others?

Whether your typical Sunday morning is chaotic or quiet, if you find yourself asking these questions, you are feeling a deep longing. It's the ache for something more, better, different— something that truly meets your expectations.

This longing is older than you realize. It's an echo all the way from the Garden of Eden, reverberating in our modern lives. It's with us as we walk through our days and every time we sit in church with distracted hearts and worried minds, craving a sense of wholeness. The ancient ache you feel isn't trivial. It's from the very beginning of human history, and it is drawing us back to our original purpose and relationship with God.

The question is *why*. The simple answer is that you were *made to worship God*. Being in relationship with God and worshiping Him is your purpose on this earth, and as I've mentioned before, I'm convinced that if you can get worship right, you will get *everything* right.

THE ANCIENT LONGING

Worship started with Adam and Eve all the way back in Genesis. If you're thinking, "Mike, I don't remember reading any passages about Adam and Eve raising their hands and singing praise choruses," you're right. There's no picture of modern worship in the Garden of Eden, or even anything resembling what we see in the Psalms. The picture in the Garden is far more beautiful than that.

The way Adam and Eve worshiped in the garden is the only time the Bible shows worship that was completely uninterrupted—just pure, direct connection with God. After that, perfect worship like theirs hasn't been seen again on earth, and it won't be seen again until Christ returns.

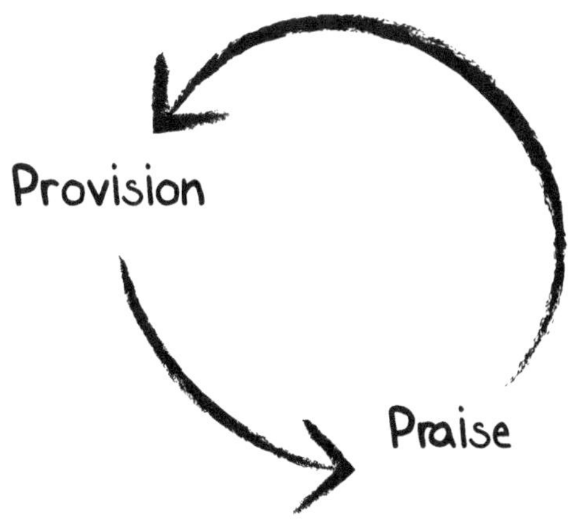

Originally, there was nothing between us and God—no interruption. The cycle of worship was simple. God provided everything we needed, and our natural response was praise—uncomplicated, satisfying, and intimate. The stars, the oceans, the mountains—they "praise" by design.

When God created Adam and Eve, He gave them and all of humanity a unique ability among His creations: the *freedom* to choose whether or not to love and worship Him. This freedom sets humans apart from the rest of creation, and that freedom is essential because real love can't be forced. Unfortunately, the power of choice also poses a problem. We can choose not to live a life of worship.

And as we know, Adam and Eve chose to disobey God. They chose their way over His, and in doing so, they created the first idol: self.

Obedience flows from our worship. When our worship is rightly placed, our desire is to do anything God asks. But if the object of our worship shifts, our obedience shifts with it, and the moment Adam and Eve disobeyed God, they interrupted the perfect cycle of worship. They invited disruption and distance into their relationship with Him.

Remember that hectic Sunday morning when you were trying to get the family to church? Now, picture a morning with no chaos, no arguments, no worries about what to wear or if there's enough gas in the tank—just communion and wholeness. That's what Adam and Eve experienced in the Garden. That's the peace and connection we exchange when we focus our worship on anything other than God.

Our everyday frustrations, the sense of being just a little out of sync, that longing for wholeness and fulfillment are the result of an interrupted cycle, and the way to return is to worship, again.

Disobedience separated Adam and Eve from God. The very next thing they did was hide from God. It disrupted their relationship.

But in that disruption, we immediately see God do something remarkable. He goes looking for them. He calls out to them. Even in their shame, God seeks to restore the relationship and makes coverings for Adam and Eve because He still desires a relationship with them (Genesis 3:21).

But because of their sin, Adam and Eve were sent out of the Garden. If choosing to worship inside paradise was a struggle, then choosing to worship outside the Garden will require a different kind of resolve. It is no longer natural. Now it is contested.What was once a simple, natural relationship, where God provided and we responded with praise and satisfaction, became fractured. Now, there are choices, distractions, competing desires, and obstacles that make returning to a worshiping relationship with God a challenge.

From this point on, we start to see intentional acts of worship throughout the Bible: building altars, bringing sacrifices, and other expressions of devotion continuing into our lives today. Just one generation after Adam and Eve, their sons Cain and Abel offered the first sacrifices to God, as recorded in Genesis 4:3–4.

Cain brought the fruits of his harvest, while Abel brought the firstborn of his flock—the costly portion, the best he had.

And while this scene still doesn't look like what we might call "worship" today, it highlights something essential that has never changed: the posture of the heart matters most.

One offering was convenient. The other was costly. One said, "Here is what I can spare." The other said, "I honor You with my first and my best." In this first picture of worship after Eden, true worship is not measured by the form of the offering but by the heart behind it—by whether our gift reflects convenience or surrender, leftover affection or wholehearted devotion. This moment sets the tone for all worship that follows.[1]

Every time we try to prepare our hearts for worship and instead feel distance, a wandering mind, or a cold heart, we're experiencing the same distance first introduced in the Garden. It's the ache for the intimacy we were designed for, the intimacy Adam and Eve once knew.

We can't undo the disobedience, and we can't go back to the perfect conditions of the Garden, but we can reconnect with our original purpose and engage in worship the way God desires.

We will dive deep into the different methods and practices of worship throughout this book, but I want you to know that no matter what is going on in your life or your relationship with God, you were made to worship—and you don't need to fit someone else's vision of worship to draw closer to God.

---

[1]   See Appendix A: "Old Testament Expressions of Worship – and the Rise of Davidic Worship" for a fuller overview of how worship develops in the Old Testament.

REASONS TO WORSHIP

What moves us to worship even when our hearts feel distant or distracted? David, in Psalm 145, pours out his heart in praise, giving voice to the many reasons that draw us toward God. He's not just performing a ritual. David's worship is an authentic response, a conversation with the living God filled with awe, gratitude, and longing.

David was not a perfect man, but he provides a model of getting worship right on this side of the Garden. He shows us what it looks like to live a lifestyle of worship that most closely resembles the heart of Eden—imperfect but deeply connected. And this isn't just because of what David says in his songs and prayers but because of what God Himself says about him—that David is "a man after [God's] own heart" (1 Samuel 13:14; Acts 13:22).

Based on Psalm 145, here are some of the reasons David shares about why he worships.

> **God's Greatness.** David begins with God's greatness: "Great is the LORD and most worthy of praise; his greatness no one can fathom" (v. 3). It feels like he's standing at the edge of something immeasurable, trying to capture wonder in words. Have you ever found yourself awestruck by a sunrise, a work of art? David reminds us that real worship springs from recognizing that God's nature is far beyond our grasp, inspiring reverence that is deeper than words.

God's Mighty Acts. David recounts the "wonderful works" and "mighty acts" (vv. 4–5) that fill creation with evidence of God's power and involvement in history. Gratitude wells up as he considers what God has done—not just in the stories of the past but in his own life. When was the last time you paused to reflect on answered prayers, moments of provision, or unexpected guidance? Worship is renewed as we recall God's far-reaching care.

God's Abundant Goodness. David also praises the Lord for being "gracious and compassionate" and "rich in love" (v. 8). Think of a moment when someone's kindness changed your day. These qualities, expressed in God's dealings with us, are an invitation to respond with love and gratitude. Even when we feel the ache or emptiness of distance from him, God's goodness meets us with grace.

God's Faithfulness. David proclaims, "The LORD is trustworthy in all he promises and faithful in all he does" (v. 13). Generation after generation, God keeps His word. In times of uncertainty or disappointment, worship can anchor us in the security of God's faithfulness, reminding us we're not alone and that His promises hold even when all else shifts.

God's Nearness. Perhaps most comforting is that God's nearness is crucial. "The Lord is near to all who call on him, to all who call on him in truth" (v. 18). In moments of need and longing, God hears our cries, meets us with compassion, and draws us close. That sense of belonging is the heart of true worship, a taste of the intimacy we were created for.

The reasons to worship God are endless, but I love what Psalm 145 models.

Worship has the power to bring us closer to God and help us find that connection we've been longing for since Eden. Why do we worship? Because God is great, He performs mighty acts, He is good, He is faithful, and He wants us to draw near to Him. While we may never fully recapture the perfect harmony that Adam and Eve knew, we are still invited to seek and encounter our Creator through worship. Of all the things we do in God's name, worship alone is eternal—the one act that continues now and forever, linking us with heaven even in our most ordinary moments.

THE ETERNAL NATURE OF WORSHIP

Missions, evangelism, and discipleship all have a profound and meaningful purpose, but as I said, if we get worship right—if we truly desire God above all—we will get everything else right.

Missions will one day be complete. Evangelism will one day cease. Discipleship will find its fulfillment. But worship—the adoration of God, the lifting of His name, the response of our hearts to His glory—will continue forever.

We may not know every detail of what heaven will be like, but Scripture makes clear that worship will be its heartbeat—pure, endless, undistracted praise. In Revelation 4 and 5, we see angelic beings and elders fall before God's radiant throne, proclaiming His holiness and creative power. When Jesus the Lamb appears, every being in heaven breaks out in thunderous praise.

One day, all our earthly striving will come to an end, but worship will remain (Philippians 2:10–11). Across every age and circumstance, worship has endured. It survived Eden's loss and brokenness, it continues with us here and now, and ultimately it will remain as the eternal song of those gathered around God's throne.

THE INTERRUPTED CYCLE OF WORSHIP

Despite our longing for the perfect intimacy Adam and Eve experienced in Eden, our relationship with God today follows a repeated, sometimes turbulent path. Below you can see the new pattern we have all entered: the Interrupted Cycle of Worship.

At the heart of it, you still see the intended design, the perfect relationship with God, His provision, and the satisfaction and praise that Adam and Eve returned to Him until they disobeyed Him.

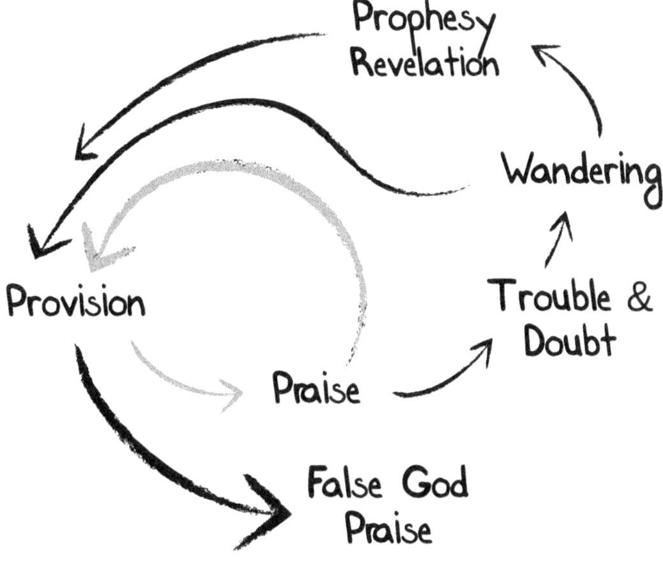

After sin entered the picture, that relationship was damaged, but worship didn't disappear or become irrelevant. In fact, the opposite happened.

Worship became more important than ever. It became a conscious act performed by sinners to draw themselves near to God. The new cycle not only includes provision and praise but also new paths introduced by Adam and Eve's disobedience— interruptions like troubled times, doubt, wandering, and false gods that can pull our hearts away from the One who created it all.

And yet even with these interruptions, *God hasn't changed.* His desire is still the same: a relationship we willingly choose to have with Him. God is seeking worshipers—true worshipers— those who choose Him, not out of obligation but out of love (John 4:23).

No matter how far we've wandered or how distant God feels, worship is how we return to Him. When we worship again, we walk the same path God's people have walked for generations and realign our hearts with His presence.

You don't need to be perfect before you start the journey back to God. Worship doesn't require us to have it all together. It simply leads us back, inviting us into renewed intimacy, reminding us that God's invitation is always open and that He is all we need.

It's the beauty of the Prodigal Son. The Father is always waiting and hoping for your return.

Each turn through the cycle reflects our ongoing spiritual journey like a dance between nearness and distance, provision and response, disruption and restoration. Ultimately, the invitation is to choose to worship again, even in our wandering.

WHY IT MATTERS

This cycle is not a sign of failure but a picture of grace. It explains why choosing to worship may feel hard, because the truth is that it's easy to break the perfect cycle. Sometimes we simply want what we want. Sometimes life hits us with something we didn't choose. But whatever the reason, God's invitation remains the same.

Whenever you feel far from God, remember this: Worship is how you find your way back. The circular nature means there is always a route back from trouble, doubt, or distraction—back to God, His presence, and His provision. Let this reminder reshape the way you approach the realities of life, whether it's the chaos of a Sunday morning or an ordinary moment in your day. You were made for worship, and the journey—complete with interruptions and returns—is part of the story God is writing with your life.

RETURNING FROM LESSER LOVES

"If it's so simple, then why is it so hard?"

There are seasons when it seems worship doesn't bring fulfillment. What should draw us nearer to God leaves us empty, distracted, or yearning for something else. Imagine singing in church but the songs don't stir you, and the words feel empty. Maybe it's in your prayers. You try to reach for God, seeking healing or joy, but encounter only silence. The ache for something greater isn't merely an emotional hiccup. It's a spiritual longing with nowhere to go, hungry for connection. And you're not the first one to feel it.

In Exodus 32, it took the Israelites mere minutes—even after witnessing miracle after miracle—to build a golden calf and call it their god. They had watched God split the Red Sea. They had eaten bread from heaven and drunk water from a rock. Provision after provision. And yet in one brief moment of waiting, they turned to worship something they made with their own hands.

The longing to worship will not stay idle, and it's in moments of waiting that we sometimes choose to worship lesser loves. If our worship isn't purposefully directed to God, it doesn't disappear. It finds a new target. It will reach for lesser things to find a sense of meaning, comfort, or control.

When the worship we were made for falters, we seek idols such as success, approval, achievement, relationships, romance, and even religion itself. These can become stand-ins for God as we give them the energy, affection, and focus intended for Him.

Scripture speaks directly to this pattern. Paul writes:

> *They exchanged the truth about God for a lie,*
> *and worshiped and served created things rather*
> *than the Creator—who is forever praised. Amen.*
>
> **—ROMANS 1:25**

Whenever our worship goes sideways and we depend on created things to give us value or security, we mirror Adam and Eve, reaching for fulfillment apart from God.

Jeremiah echoes the same lament:

> *Has a nation ever changed its gods? (Yet they are*
> *not gods at all.) But my people have exchanged*
> *their glorious God for worthless idols.*
>
> **—JEREMIAH 2:11**

It's not wrong to value your relationships, success, or comfort. But when we look to these to satisfy our deepest longings above God, we choose to create distance between us. It's rarely intentional. We don't even recognize it's happening until our worship feels fractured, we're exhausted and disappointed, and we have the nagging sense that we are missing something that we truly need.

The story you've been living—of Sunday chaos, distraction, longing for connection—goes back to the interrupted cycle of worship. You try to worship, but you feel the gap, and if you aren't careful, you keep filling it with anything but God. The good news is that every moment of misdirected worship can become a turning point.

Recognizing when your heart is wandering is itself an invitation. God has not abandoned you. He is the only constant in the cycle—always there, always providing, and always desiring His creation to enjoy His presence. He remains ready to restore and draw your attention back to Himself. The call is always to return—to surrender your lesser loves and realign your heart to Him.

THE FIRST INVITATION

None of us can step into this kind of worship on our own. Before we can live a life of worship, something far more foundational has to be restored.

I want to pause and speak directly to something essential. I've spent this chapter talking about your design—why you were created, what you were made for, and how worship is the center of it all. But because of sin, there is one thing none of us can fix on our own: being made right with God.

To truly worship, we must first be in right relationship with Him. And the only way that happens is through Jesus.

Jesus lived the perfect life we could not live, died the death we deserved, and rose again so we could be forgiven, restored, and brought back into the relationship we were created for. Worship begins with that relationship. It begins with grace. It begins with Jesus.

So this invitation is for anyone who has never made the decision to put their faith in Him. If you feel the longing, if you feel the distance, if you feel the ache to be restored, this is your invitation.

Scripture makes the way clear:

> *If you declare with your mouth, "Jesus is Lord,"*
> *and believe in your heart that God raised him*
> *from the dead, you will be saved.*
>
> **—ROMANS 10:9**

This is where worship starts: by receiving the free gift of salvation and choosing the relationship God created you for.

A PRAYER FROM THE LONGING HEART

Father,

You are worthy of all praise, the Creator who instilled in us a longing for Your presence. In our busy days and restless hearts, remind us of the peace and closeness You intended for us to have with You from the beginning.

Forgive us, Lord, for letting distractions and lesser loves draw our worship away from You. Thank You for Your faithfulness, Your goodness, and Your nearness when we call. Restore our sense of wonder and gratitude, and help us return to worship—not just as routine but as a genuine response to Your greatness.

Meet us in our longing, and rekindle in us a love that freely chooses You. Let our worship anchor us in Your presence, now and always.

Amen.

Before we wrap up this chapter, you'll find a short section called "Unpacking Worship Realities." You'll see this at the end of each chapter. In these pages, I'll briefly address common questions, tensions, or misunderstandings about worship that many of us wonder but don't always say out loud—so you can process what you've just read in a clear, practical way.

UNPACKING WORSHIP REALITIES

Why does God even need our worship? He's all-powerful. What can my worship do for Him?

I love this question. On the surface, it seems hard to answer, but in reality, it's simple. Why does God need our worship?

He doesn't.

He *wants* it. He *desires* it because He desires *us*. But He doesn't *need* it.

God created us to have a relationship with Him, and He gives us the profound gift of choice in how we respond. While God needs nothing from us, He desires love returned freely, which again is the only way true love can be demonstrated.

Remember the perfect worship cycle Adam and Eve shared with Him? He provided for them because He loved them. They worshiped Him to show their gratitude and love in return.

This analogy won't completely do it justice, but think about your friendships. Imagine that you're the friend always reaching out, calling, texting, or trying to make plans to get together. You hope your interest in your friends and efforts to be in a relationship with them will be returned because one-sided relationships feel bad.

Maybe that friend is just clueless or going through a difficult season of life, but that hope for reciprocation is real. On a much grander and deeper scale, this is the relationship God wants with us.

He provides because He loves us, and He continues to do that no matter what we do. In return, we have the choice to reciprocate that love.

Worship is the unique method created for us to love God back. It's not forced, but invited. Our choice to worship makes the relationship real and meaningful, not mechanical.

God's desire for worship isn't limited to an hour on Sundays either. He longs for continual, day-by-day intimacy.

Ultimately, God wants us to experience life as it was meant to be—anchored by love, guided by gratitude, and aligned with His purposes. Our worship, freely given, glorifies God and opens space for a deeper, more intimate relationship where true love is experienced and returned.

I will exalt you, my God the King;
I will praise your name for ever and ever.
Every day I will praise you
and extol your name for ever and ever.
Great is the Lord and most worthy of praise;
his greatness no one can fathom.

One generation commends your works
to another;
they tell of your mighty acts.
They speak of the glorious splendor of
your majesty—
and I will meditate on your wonderful works.
They tell of the power of your awesome works—
and I will proclaim your great deeds.
They celebrate your abundant goodness
and joyfully sing of your righteousness.

The Lord is gracious and compassionate,
slow to anger and rich in love.
The Lord is good to all;
he has compassion on all he has made.

All your works praise you, Lord;
your faithful people extol you.
They tell of the glory of your kingdom
and speak of your might,
so that all people may know of your mighty acts
and the glorious splendor of your kingdom.

Your kingdom is an everlasting kingdom,
and your dominion endures through all
generations.

The Lord is trustworthy in all he promises
and faithful in all he does.
The Lord upholds all who fall
and lifts up all who are bowed down.

The eyes of all look to you,
and you give them their food at the proper time.
You open your hand
and satisfy the desires of every living thing.

The Lord is righteous in all his ways
and faithful in all he does.
The Lord is near to all who call on him,
to all who call on him in truth.
He fulfills the desires of those who fear him;
he hears their cry and saves them.
The Lord watches over all who love him,
but all the wicked he will destroy.

My mouth will speak in praise of the Lord.
Let every creature praise his holy name
for ever and ever.

PSALM 145:1–21

I have come that they may have
life, and have it to the full.

JOHN 10:10

REIMAGINE: WHAT WORSHIP TRULY IS

rue worship changes lives. That's why I feel so passionately about bringing this message of worship to as many people as I can. Worship isn't meant to be just a Sunday ritual, a special music set, or a tradition you only revisit on holidays. At its heart, worship is the choice to center everything—time, energy, relationships, struggles, and joy—around God, letting Him occupy the highest place in every day. When that shift happens, life is transformed from the inside out.

Imagine stepping into a Monday where God isn't just present in the prayers you remember to pray in the morning but in the commute, the tense conversation, the tired dinner, or the quiet walk after sunset. Worship draws heaven into those ordinary places, inviting God's presence, peace, and purpose to fill even what seems routine.

Suddenly, your career, your friendships, and your choices are not just tasks or obligations. They become opportunities to live the abundant life Jesus promised—a life marked by joy, resilience, and meaning that the world can't steal.

Worship unlocks growth in patience, love, hope, and freedom, even when circumstances are hard. It is this posture, returning and realigning, that brings fulfillment. Life becomes more vivid, relationships become more meaningful, and your purpose becomes clearer.

Where we once felt stuck or empty, we begin to overflow. Where we once held back, we find ourselves drawn into something bigger and better than we imagined. Worship, in the way God intends, makes life whole and invites us to live it to the very fullest.

But this kind of life—overflowing, vibrant, and centered on God—doesn't just happen automatically. For most of us, the way we live and the way we worship has been shaped by experiences, traditions, and unnoticed influences. Before we can step fully into this abundant life, it's worth asking, *How did we get here? How did we learn what worship is, and who taught us what it looks like?*

Whether our first lessons came from parents, friends, church routines, or even our own hunger for meaning, our understanding of worship is a story in itself—sometimes clear, sometimes confusing, sometimes left with gaps or assumptions. To discover what's possible, we need to honestly look at where we started, how our practices took shape, and which patterns have held us back or drawn us closer.

Let's pause and trace our worship story—looking for God's invitation not just in the destination but in every part of the journey so far.

THE HUMAN APPROACH

Who taught you about worship? Did you take a class? Have discussions in youth group? Pick up cues from the worship leader during Sunday services? If so, I would guess that you fall into one of three categories:

1. You grew up in church. Worship was always part of the experience. You learned to worship the same way children learn to talk. You watched, listened, copied, received feedback, and eventually learned the language of worship through participating with others.

If this is you, I imagine you didn't ask many questions about what you were doing and why. This isn't a criticism. It's natural to simply accept the things we learn at a young age. You probably don't question why we wave to people when we see them because you've done it your whole life. It's natural. It's just what you do.

2. You *didn't* grow up in church. You learned about worship later in life as a teen or an adult. Learning how to worship might have felt like learning a foreign language—uncomfortable, strange, sometimes embarrassing. You had to go through the experience of watching, listening, imitating, and receiving feedback with the self-consciousness we often develop with age.

It's difficult for us to be new at something when we're older, but you persevered and learned the language of worship. You might have been bold enough to question why you were doing something or how it was supposed to look. I wonder if your questions were answered well. I wonder if you held back questions because you didn't want to rock the boat or seem like you didn't know what was going on.

3. You're a combination of one and two. You grew up in church and learned about worship by being immersed in it at services. It was always part of church life, and you accepted it. And then one day you asked yourself, "Why? Why do we spend the first half of the services singing songs? Why do some people raise their hands? What is the point of it all?"

It can be intimidating to ask questions about the fundamentals of something people assume you already understand. Sometimes we do things we know are good, worthy, and important, but we can't truly articulate why, what, or how.

The reality is that no matter how we learned about worship—whether by absorbing it from childhood, discovering it as adults, or some mix of both—our understanding is often shaped by incomplete experiences, secondhand assumptions, and sometimes unanswered questions.

Simply put, we learn about worship from other humans who experience the same interrupted worship, so it's no wonder we have such a hard time understanding it.

We've been looking for methods to worship God ever since Adam and Eve disobeyed and broke the perfect cycle of worship. And the last few decades have been fixated on music as its source when there is much more to explore and enjoy.

As we walk through these pages, we'll expand and open up worship opportunities in every moment of our lives. *Reworship* is a word that carries an invitation to worship again, to return to true worship, not just familiar routines. But first, we need to lay a solid foundation. We're starting an honest exploration of worship basics that will shape our lives, our families, our communities, and our relationship with God moving forward. And we're asking, "What is really at the highest place in my life?"

WHAT IS WORSHIP?

We devote much time and energy to our worship services. Many churches hire worship leaders whose main job is overseeing the worship service. They organize worship teams and choirs, and then all those people spend time and energy preparing for the services. And they couldn't make any of it happen without the audio and video teams. Then there's the congregation—the people who come and participate and bring their hearts, souls, and voices to worship. There's even an entire music industry based on worship.

So if I asked you to define *worship*, could you?

Take a second and try. Don't worry if your answer is no or the definition you come up with doesn't seem right. Sometimes it's hard to put an experience into words.

One reason worship can feel hard to define is that we often swing between two extremes, either making it only about what happens in a service or stretching it so wide that it loses shape. D. A. Carson, Emeritus Professor of New Testament, points out that the New Testament won't let us do either. Worship is no longer just an event, but it also isn't so vague that the gathered people of God stop mattering. Scripture holds both together: a whole life offered to God and a people who intentionally gather in response to Him.[2]

When we talk about worship, we often think first of church or spiritual reverence. But the word *worship* actually has broader and older roots. Its origin comes from the Old English "worth-ship," meaning the act of ascribing worth to something.

In other words, it means assigning value, giving honor, and elevating something—or someone—to a place of importance in our lives. Notice that there is no mention of music in that definition, and it doesn't limit worship to Sunday mornings or sacred spaces. We all ascribe worth to things—sometimes to careers, relationships, celebrities, sports, comfort, success, or even religion or church itself.

In light of this, here is my definition: *Worship is the orientation and surrendering of your entire life around what you value most.*

Worship reveals itself day after day in whatever claims your focus, directs your choices, and sets the shape of your routines and relationships. Over time, the term has become most closely associated with reverence for God, but it wasn't always that way.

Its foundational meaning is still true, and it points to a deeper truth: everyone worships something. Realizing this, worship becomes not just an event but the guiding pursuit of life. Pastor Timothy Keller puts it this way: "Everybody has to live for something, and if you do not live for God, you will live

---

[2] See D. A. Carson's discussion of worship under the new covenant in *Worship by the Book* (Grand Rapids, MI: Zondervan, 2002).

for something else. Whatever that something else is will drive you, shape you, and ultimately enslave you."[3]

It's not only about what you say you value; it's about your deepest loyalties and the driving force behind your choices. The real question becomes this: *What's truly at the top of my priorities—what does the rest of my life organize itself around?*

In answering that, we begin to see who or what we really worship.

Take a moment to consider the top three things that capture most of your time, energy, and attention during a typical week. It could be people, activities, goals, a job, your phone, or something else. Don't overthink it; just pick whatever comes to mind first.

If you're truly stuck, taking a glance at your calendar or weekly schedule might shine a light on where your hours and attention really go.

Consider your list of three priorities. What does it reveal about what or who is receiving your time, energy, and affection?

Maybe your list includes driving kids to practice, making dinner, and squeezing in walks with the dog. Or maybe your week is full of work projects, meetings, and constant emails. For others, the rhythms revolve around workouts and meal prep. For most of us, it's some combination of all the above—full weeks shaped by real responsibilities and good things that matter.

This exercise isn't meant to accuse or shame you. It is simply meant to help you notice the state of your priorities. The way you spend your time and energy doesn't condemn you, but it does

---

3   Timothy Keller, *The Reason for God: Belief in an Age of Skepticism* (New York: Dutton, 2008), 163.

tell the truth about where your attention is most often pulled. Many of those things are good gifts and real responsibilities God has entrusted to you.

So the question isn't "Where does God fit into all of this?" The question is "Where is He seated in it—does He hold the highest place, above everything else?"

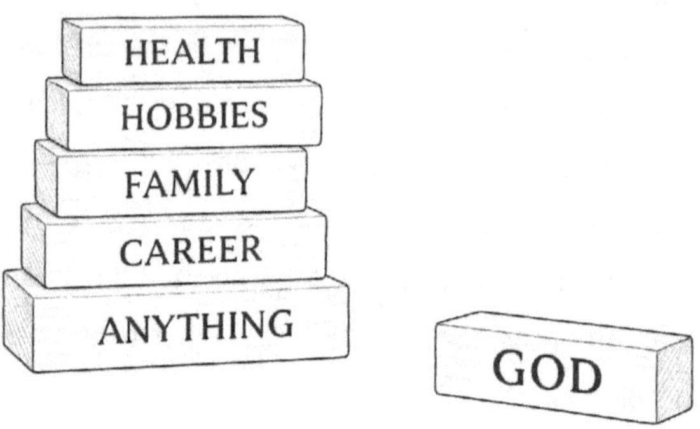

Imagine a stack of blocks—a vertical tower where everything you value is set one above another. Your job, family, health, friends, and hobbies each has a place in this stack according to the attention, energy, and devotion you give it. The higher in the stack, the more value you ascribe to it.

But only one thing can be at the very top. That top spot determines the value and priority of everything else. If you build your stack with God at the highest point—above every other gift, responsibility, or passion—then everything else slides into place beneath that. Everything else benefits from the trickle-down of God at the top. Worship becomes whole, and your energy, time, and priorities align in a way that brings fulfillment and peace.

But if anything, no matter how worthy, finds its way to the top instead of God, your stack is out of order. Worship loses its wholeness, and life feels scattered or empty—maybe not at first, but time has a way of revealing disorder, unfulfillment, and an uneasy distance from Him.

You can value many things, and it's good to care deeply about what matters in your life. The other items in your stack aren't worthless. Many things like family deserve a high place in your stack, but the challenge is to set God above all—giving Him the place of greatest influence—so your worship flows naturally, and every other gift is held as it should be. When God isn't at the top, worship gets interrupted, distracted, or diminished, and our hearts sense that something essential is missing.

WHEN LIFE IS OUT OF ORDER

Imagine Sarah, a devoted churchgoer and mother of two. She cares deeply about her faith, attends Sunday services regularly, and volunteers whenever she can. But during the week, her attention is consumed by work deadlines, her kids' activities, and the constant buzz of her phone.

Mornings start with emails, not prayer. Evenings wind down with Netflix, not gratitude. She tells herself she'll make time for God later, maybe after this busy season, but there's always something urgent that needs her focus.

Over time, Sarah notices that her faith feels stale. Worship services feel like she's going through the motions, her prayers are distracted, and she's more anxious and lonely. When troubles come, she wonders why God feels distant.

But God hasn't left her. He always provides even when we fall into distraction. She had unintentionally moved God down in her stack. Sarah's story is not about outright rebellion. It's simply that her attention, time, and energy are ordered in a way that puts good things—family, career, comfort—ahead of the One who gives them meaning. She's worshiping, but the order is off, and the result is emptiness, restlessness, and a longing for something more.

Worship is much more than music. In later chapters, we will dive deeply into the expansiveness of worship. But for now, I want you to know this: Worship is our only proper response to God in an ongoing cycle of receiving from and returning to Him as the One who belongs at the top of our priorities.

Think back to the Cycle of Worship that we looked at in Chapter 1. God offers His presence and provision; we are satisfied, and we worship in response.

Now consider the way relationships unfold in our daily lives. Think of a close friendship, a marriage, or a bond between parent and child. Healthy relationships take time, effort, attention, and deliberate prioritization.

Connection is deepened by simple, daily choices—picking up the phone just to check in, remembering milestones, sharing both joys and struggles, and practicing forgiveness. What keeps the relationship alive is not a single grand gesture but an ongoing series of small, authentic efforts to return, reconnect, and value the other person above lesser distractions.

Picture what happens when these relationships slip out of order. Imagine a marriage where work or hobbies take precedence, leaving little space for conversation or joy together. The love may still exist, but the connection withers, replaced by routine or even resentment.

Or think of a friendship that only comes alive in moments of crisis where there's little genuine exchange until trouble strikes. We reach out, not from a place of joy or love but from necessity, hoping for comfort or rescue. In both cases, the relationship suffers, not because of a single mistake but because it is no longer held as a priority.

Worship works much the same way. We are made for ongoing relationships and intimacy with God, but as in human relationships, we can easily put other things, even good things, above God, letting our relationship with Him become background noise. Worship becomes routine, something we drift to on Sundays or when we feel empty or desperate. We may intellectually affirm God's importance, but our days reveal a different order.

It's easy to fall into patterns where God gets whatever time is left over instead of our first attention, moving down the stack. This is disordered worship. It isn't necessarily about bad intentions. It's the result of how distraction, comfort, or busyness gradually reconfigures our priorities. As with any other relationship that's drifting due to neglect, our relationship with God can feel empty, unfulfilling, or stuck when He is no longer at the top.

What can you do when your worship becomes disordered? God's grace plays a big role here. When we're distracted, He does not stop providing. He does not hold a grudge. There is always a way back—an invitation to reconnect, reprioritize, and restore your closeness with God.

In the cycle of worship, the way back to intimacy with God is to worship *again*. Just as reaching out to an old friend begins with a simple call, returning to true worship can begin with a prayer, an act of gratitude, or a reminder that God's love waits patiently for our return.

ABRAHAM'S WORSHIP

The first time we see the word *worship* in Scripture is in Genesis 22:5. At this point, Abraham has received what he wanted most. God has fulfilled His promise. Isaac—Abraham's long-awaited son, the embodiment of hope, legacy, and future—is finally here. Everything Abraham had trusted God for now lives and breathes in front of him. And it is precisely here, at the point of fulfillment, that God tests him.

> *He said to his servants, "Stay here with the donkey while I and the boy go over there. We will worship and then we will come back to you."*
>
> **—GENESIS 22:5**

Abraham said this just before he climbed Mount Moriah with Isaac. He knew he was supposed to sacrifice his son on the mountain. God had commanded it. Why would he call that *worship*? It doesn't fit the modern practice of worship we see today.

In Abraham's case, worship was not about music or offering adoration. It was about obedience, surrendering his personal will, and trusting God's goodness, even amid painful circumstances. Even though it pained him, Abraham put God at the top and gave Him the highest worship—his trust and obedience.

Centuries later, the prophet Samuel would say it plainly: "Does the LORD delight in burnt offerings and sacrifices as much as in obeying the LORD? To obey is better than sacrifice" (1 Samuel 15:22).

Abraham's actions—gathering wood for the offering, bringing the knife, and traveling with Isaac up the mountain—demonstrate the act of surrendering to God's will. Abraham did not know how the story would end, but he trusted God and put His will above all else.

God rewarded Abraham's complete surrender and worshipful actions by sparing Isaac.

We can contrast Abraham's worship with Adam and Eve's. Though they had the perfect experience and communion with God, they put their own desires at the top. They chose to eat the fruit, even though God forbade it. They valued their desires more than God's will.

Abraham knew from the moment he started the climb with Isaac that God wanted him to sacrifice his son—and still, he climbed the mountain and prepared to do what God had asked. He is the ultimate example of putting God first and putting self last.

I love A. W. Tozer's perspective that at the core of sin is our refusal to dethrone ourselves, which is why true worship means stepping off the throne of our own lives to make room for God.

A PRAYER FROM A
SEARCHING HEART

Sometimes the journey back to true worship begins simply with a longing—a simple hope to reconnect with God. Words can help us express what our hearts are reaching for. The following prayer offers space to realign your attention and affections, inviting God to reclaim the highest place in your life.

God,

My desire is for You to be at the highest level of anything I value, honor, have affection for, or glory in. I want You to have my mind's attention and my heart's affection— more than anything else, more than any other things that You give. I want to love You the most.

Amen.

Pause after this prayer. Notice how it feels to speak those words honestly. Whether this sentiment feels familiar or brand new, remember that reordering your worship is not a one-time act but a lifelong journey. Each day is a fresh opportunity to give God your whole heart, letting everything else you value find its rightful place. Let this prayer be the start—not an end—as you continue reimagining what worship can look like in your daily life

UNPACKING WORSHIP REALITIES

Why does worship look so different at different churches?

It's a question many of us may have asked. Walk into a dozen churches—even in the same town—and you'll see a range of styles, traditions, and outward expressions of praise. Some congregations sing with bands and raised hands; others find God in quiet reflection, ancient liturgy, or creative arts. Even siblings worshiping together may connect with God differently on the outside.

So why all the variety? And is any one way the *right* way to worship?

The answer has two parts and starts with a crucial truth: Worship doesn't look any one way, because real worship starts on the inside. Before it's seen or heard, worship is a matter of orientation—how a person's heart, mind, and will turn toward God. The external forms such as music, prayer, art, and traditions are all just "wrappings" for something deeper.

It's easy to mistake the outward expressions of worship for the "important part"—judging others, or even ourselves, by what worship looks like on the outside rather than the order and devotion of the heart. The goal isn't uniformity in the way we worship but an authentic offering to God.

Now, the second part of the answer: Why does it look different on the outside?

True worship also reflects diversity. Every faith community is shaped by its own culture, history, and people—bringing unique backgrounds, generations, and personalities into its connection to God.

Every church has its own personality. None of them is ultimately right, and none of them is wrong. God didn't create us all the same, and that is why we see a rich display of style and creativity from place to place.

God's delight in this diversity is clear throughout Scripture and history. The early church broke bread and sang psalms. King David danced with abandon. Ancient Israel worshiped with feasts, poetry, lament, and celebration. Did you know that Moses led an epic battle worship song after the Israelites crossed the Red Sea? Then right after that, Miriam and others busted out a tambourine for a spontaneous praise break.

Even now, elders and children, introverts and extroverts find meaningful ways to worship that don't always look the same. What it looks like is not the important part; it is the heart that seeks God above all else. God has always cared more about the heart than the performance of worship. When our hearts are oriented on God, whatever flows outward becomes an honest expression of true worship. That's what God desires in every congregation and every life.

It's tempting to think that "real worship" must fit a certain mold, especially if that's what you're used to. It would probably even be a lot easier if it worked that way. But God, the Creator of every tongue and tribe, loves the tapestry of genuine devotion. When we embrace worship's diversity, we honor His image in every believer and discover new facets of His character.

The next time you join a worship service, allow your heart to come alive, and trust Him to handle the rest.

Therefore, I urge you, brothers
and sisters, in view of God's
mercy, to offer your bodies
as a living sacrifice, holy and
pleasing to God—this is your
true and proper worship.

ROMANS 12:1

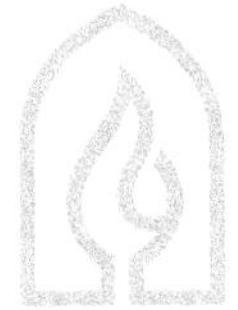

CHAPTER THREE

RECENTER: WORSHIP THROUGH DAILY LIVING

There are a million little miracles happening in people's everyday lives that go unnoticed and uncelebrated. They feel normal and mundane, so we shrug and think, "That's not a big deal." A quiet prayer whispered under your breath before a hard conversation, a friend who sends a text at just the right time, a neighbor who quietly shovels someone else's driveway—most of us would just call these "nice things," not miracles.

In the same way, when someone is working a tough job, dealing with an angry customer, and still chooses to love that person, to respect and value them, we rarely label it a miracle. But that is exactly what it is.

Our natural response would be to yell or fire back a sarcastic comment. Choosing to love and respect that person is something beyond our natural inclinations. It's a "God thing"—a characteristic of God shining through, a human being putting God's will before their own, whether a person knows it or not. Moments like that are the Spirit quietly growing God's character in us, even when we would just call it being nice.

Those kinds of miracles happen all the time, but we're often too busy to notice, or we don't think they're that special. A barista who slows down long enough to talk to a lonely regular. A spouse who chooses a gentle word instead of the perfect comeback. A parent who pauses, breathes, and listens to a child instead of snapping. These are not just personality wins or good manners. They are everyday evidence of God's love breaking into ordinary life, and they deserve to be highlighted just as much as the big signs and wonders.

The problem is that most of us have been taught to center our worship around events such as Easter Sunday, a youth conference, and Sunday mornings. We keep waiting for the next experience to feel close to God again. But if you acted that way in any of your personal relationships—waiting until the next birthday or holiday to draw closer to someone—you wouldn't have very meaningful connections. God wants to be closer than that. He is always there, present and providing, and He wants us to draw near to Him through worship.

If God has a love language, it would be worship.

What if every conversation, commute, email, conflict, and quiet moment became a way to connect with God? What if we started celebrating all these seemingly small moments as holy because we allow God to be present and active in each one?

Sometimes my inner voice whispers, "Mike, you're over-spiritualizing. You're looking for meaning where there isn't any. Being nice to someone is just being nice." But Romans 12:2 combats that cynicism: "Do not conform to the pattern of this world, but be transformed by the renewing of your mind." Learning to look for God's presence and activity in ordinary moments is not wishful thinking. It is part of how God retrains our minds to discern His "good, pleasing, and perfect will."

As our minds are renewed, we begin to recognize that these "small" acts of love, humility, and surrender are not insignificant. They are our true and proper worship, offered one ordinary moment at a time.

This chapter is about learning to see how you can live out your ordinary days as holy, recognize the presence of God, and become a living sacrifice in the middle of all the normal moments most people never think to call "worship." Recognizing the quiet, steady work of God in the middle of your Monday afternoon is one step closer to living a life of worship.

A LIVING SACRIFICE BECOMES A LIFESTYLE OF WORSHIP

When Paul talks about a "living sacrifice," he is not tossing out a poetic phrase. He is giving a concrete picture of what a whole-life response to worship actually looks like.

In the Old Testament, sacrifices were set apart, examined, and placed on the altar. Once offered, they no longer belonged to the person who brought them. They belonged entirely to God. Once given, a sacrifice could not be taken back.

To say you are a "living sacrifice" is to take that altar image and apply it to your everyday life. You still breathe, work, parent, rest, and play, but you do all of it as someone who has said to God, "My life is Yours. All of it."

The big difference here is the word *living*. God is not asking you to die on an altar. Jesus has already done that, and He rose again. He is inviting you to live a life of fulfillment and satisfaction in Him. This living sacrifice is offered again and again in everyday choices.

Picture this. You choose patience instead of entitlement when your plans are interrupted. You pause before hitting "send" and ask God if this text or email reflects His heart. You set your phone down at dinner to give your full attention to the person across from you. Being a living sacrifice isn't one grand gesture. It's these simple acts of obedience and trust that give God your whole self, one ordinary moment at a time.

A lifestyle of worship is what happens when "living sacrifice" stops being an idea and starts becoming your normal. It's not an extra layer you add to your life. It is the way you live life altogether. Instead of worship being a category alongside work, family, and rest, it becomes the posture that shapes how you work, how you love your family, how you rest, and everything in between.

Most of us were trained, intentionally or not, to think of worship as a slot on the schedule: the music before the sermon, the quiet time in the morning, the retreat on the calendar. A lifestyle of worship flips that script. It says, "All of it belongs to God—anytime, anywhere."

It is answering one big question over and over in a conversation, an email, a meeting, a decision, a conflict: *What does it look like to worship God through this?*

That means worship becomes less about "what I feel" in a worship service and more about "how I respond" to every arena of life.

A lifestyle of worship is a whole-life response to who God is and what He has done, expressed in the way you actually live. When God is leading you and you choose to obey—even when another option would be easier or more appealing—you are allowing that ordinary moment to become an act of worship. Each yes to God turns everyday life into a place where His presence is honored and magnified.

If you choose integrity when cutting a corner would be easier, that is worship. When you forgive instead of nursing resentment, that is worship. When you bring God into a business decision, pause to ask for wisdom with your kids, or quietly serve someone who can't repay you, that is worship.

It is also deeply relational. It's not God demanding constant performance. It is intimacy and fellowship with God that renews you.

Think of it as walking through the day with an awareness that He is with you and shaping your choices around that presence. Over time, this reshapes your instincts. You begin to think, "How can I delight God here?" not only, "What do I want?" Everything from your doctor's appointment to your wait in the school pick-up line slowly begins to say the same thing: "God, work in my life—I'm living for You, and my desire is to please You."

None of this happens overnight. A lifestyle of worship grows the same way any relationship grows—through intentional, repeated, imperfect, honest attempts. Sometimes you will forget. You may default to old patterns or even get it wrong. But every time you turn your attention back to God in the middle of your regular life, you are practicing worship. You are training your heart to live as a living sacrifice, a true worshiper, beyond Sunday.

EVERY MOMENT IS HOLY

"We ought not to be weary of doing little things for the love of God, who regards not the greatness of the work, but the love with which it is performed."[4]

Most of us carry an invisible chart in our heads that ranks certain moments as "spiritual" and others as "just life." Church services, worship concerts, and quiet times go in the "holy" column. Commutes, laundry, emails, grocery runs, and bedtime routines go in the "ordinary" column. Without realizing it, we start to believe God is mostly interested in the first list and mostly absent from the second.

But if God is always present everywhere, then there is no such thing as a God-free zone in your day. His presence does not clock in when the worship music starts and clock out when you pull out of the church parking lot. We've placed limits on where we can worship and connect with God.

The same Spirit who moves in a sanctuary is with you in your kitchen, in your car, in your office, and at the ball field.

---

4   Brother Lawrence, *The Practice of the Presence of God*, trans. John J. Delaney (Garden City, NY: Image Books, 1977), 78.

The disconnect is not God's presence. It's that we put our ability to worship and connect with God in those slots on the schedule. We must choose to be aware of His presence all the time, everywhere we go.

Seeing every moment as holy means learning to live awake and responsive to the reality that God is already there—wherever you are, whatever you're doing. And if you're aware of His presence, then you can respond.

A walk around your neighborhood becomes an invitation to talk with Him. A hard conversation becomes a chance to rely on His wisdom instead of just your own. Washing dishes becomes a quiet space to thank Him or intercede for someone. The activities stay ordinary, but the awareness becomes sacred.

That is why the idea of a "lifestyle of worship" matters so much. If worship is only what happens in a church building or with a worship playlist on, most of your life will feel spiritually empty. But when you begin to treat each part of your day as a place where God can be acknowledged and glorified, the lines between "holy" and "ordinary" start to blur.

Everyone is human. We can aim for a lifestyle of worship and still miss it on an ordinary Tuesday. If you have kids, you already know not every moment feels holy. Some feel more like "Holy cow, please, send help!" Yet it is often in those chaotic, anything-but-holy-feeling moments that God invites us back to His presence and to the choice of worship.

ROMANS 12: A GUIDE FOR YOUR DAY

Right now, you might be thinking, "This sounds great, but how do I get started, and what can I do when I fall short?"

Let's get practical. What if we take Romans 12 to provide a compass for our day? Here's a simple and effective guide to live your days in worship from start to finish.

Morning: Offer your day. At the start of the day, Romans 12:1 invites you to do something very concrete: "offer your bodies as a living sacrifice, holy and pleasing to God." It may sound formal or even overwhelming, but ultimately, what this means is giving your actions, your words, your calendar, and your energy to God.

This can happen in a simple prayer.

God,

Because of who You are, my desire today is to live as a living sacrifice—holy and pleasing to You. My life is Yours. My body, my thoughts, my words, my schedule, my relationships, my decisions—use all of it in Your way. Help me do things in Your order, the way You desire, not my way but Yours.

Amen.

You're not promising to be perfect. God already knows you won't be. You're putting yourself in a posture of worship that can shape the way you move throughout the day. You may drift. You may lose sight of God's presence in your daily moments, but in starting your day by offering your life to God, you know where home is if you drift away.

Midday: Renew your mind. As the day unfolds, the pull to "conform to the pattern of this world" shows up fast—in stress, hurry, comparison, distraction, and self-protection Midday is a natural moment to pause and let your mind "be transformed by the renewing of your mind" (Romans 12:2).

That might look like taking sixty seconds to breathe and pray, "Remind me who You are and who I am." You could keep a verse on your lock screen or in a Bible app you can glance at between meetings, or tuck a small devotional or printed verse card where you'll see it in the car or at your desk. It could be a short walk with God on your lunch break or a quick reset in the car before the next obligation. The point is not length. The point is turning your attention back to God so His voice is louder than everything else.

Evening: Reflect with God. At the end of the day, Romans 12 offers a gentle way to look back—not alone and in shame but with God and with an open heart.

Thank Him for the places you saw His guidance, and recognize places you missed it. This kind of reflection is part of to "test and approve what God's will is—his good, pleasing and perfect will" (Romans 12:2). Here, you are listening to God's voice. You are letting God interpret your day, not just your own inner critic.

Over time, this simple rhythm—offering yourself in the morning, renewing your mind midday, reflecting with God at night—trains your heart to see the whole day as worship.

Romans 12:1–2 stops being two famous verses on a page and starts becoming a pattern you can actually live. There will be ups and downs, but if you take it one day at a time, you'll be surprised by how quickly you begin to see God in everyday moments.

BIBLICAL PORTRAITS OF LIFESTYLE WORSHIP

Scripture gives us example after example of people who worshiped, but the ultimate example of living a lifestyle of worship is Jesus Himself. Jesus didn't just talk about worship. He showed us how to live a life of worship. The Gospels describe Him slipping away to quiet places to pray and then returning with a clear sense of the Father's will—even when His obedience confused His closest friends.

He walked in constant intimacy and trust, letting the Father's voice set His pace, His priorities, and His responses to people. His public ministry was full of moments that could have turned into self-promotion and taking the glory for Himself. He raised the dead, turned water into wine, fed the five thousand, and always returned the credit and glory to God. When people wanted to crown Him king, He refused. He always kept the Father at the top of His stack.

Jesus' lifestyle of worship showed up in the in-between spaces as much as in the headline moments. He noticed the woman who touched His cloak in a crowd. He paused for children when the disciples saw them as a nuisance. He shared meals with people others avoided.

Worship for Jesus was not confined to the synagogue or the mountaintop. It was woven into how He walked, listened, ate, healed, taught, and even suffered. His whole life said, "Not my will, but yours be done" (Luke 22:42).

I know Jesus left some big sandals to fill. He was the Son of God who lived a sinless life and conquered death and the grave. How can we live up to *that*?

Let's talk about Daniel and Joseph, two of my favorite Bible characters. One of the reasons I love their stories so much is that they demonstrate what a lifestyle of worship actually looked like in real, ordinary life—not in ideal conditions, not in spiritual environments, but in places marked by pressure, injustice, and long seasons when obedience felt quiet and unseen.

Joseph was the favored son, but his story unfolded almost entirely in situations he did not choose—betrayed by his brothers, sold into slavery, falsely accused, imprisoned, and forgotten. Yet at every step, he chose faithfulness to God when compromise would have been easier.

In Potiphar's house, Joseph worked with integrity and refused sexual temptation, even though saying no landed him in prison where he served, interpreted dreams, and gave God the credit instead of using his gift to make a name for himself. When he finally stood before Pharaoh, he did not claim brilliance. He gave God the glory for his dream interpretations. His faithfulness in both obscurity and authority was a life of worship just as much as his ultimate leadership in the palace.

Daniel showed the same kind of whole-life devotion in a foreign empire. Taken from his home as a young man, given a new name, and trained in Babylonian culture, Daniel still oriented his entire life around God. He resisted the king's food when it would have defiled him, while still serving excellently in his role. He continued to pray three times a day, even when it became illegal, knowing it could cost him his life. He interpreted dreams and visions with clarity but consistently redirected credit to God instead of polishing his own image. And his faithfulness saw him through the lions' den.

Jesus in Galilee, Joseph in Egypt, Daniel in Babylon—all three showed that a lifestyle of worship is possible anywhere. They worshiped God in obscurity and in prominence, in suffering and in influence, in quiet obedience and in visible leadership. Their stories remind us that worship is not mainly about where you are or what you're doing. It is about whose voice you obey in the moment you are facing.

FROM EXTRAORDINARY TO EVERYDAY

You may never face a lion's den, false imprisonment, or crowds clamoring to crown you king or queen. Your battles aren't with Goliath or a golden calf, but they are still opportunities to draw nearer to God. Your life may not look like these famous biblical figures, but you still have the choice to bring God into every moment of your day.

You don't get to see your life in hindsight like you do the lives of Jesus, Joseph, and Daniel. You do get to make decisions to say yes to God and His way every day. In all your stories, you can live a life surrendered to God.

You never know what small moment is really a door opening. Every day brings its own crossroads, but the pattern holds the same. Surrendering my way for God's way—even if the stakes are small—unlocks fullness of life. The size of the circumstance doesn't change the size of the choice.

A lifestyle is the foundation that all our familiar pictures of worship stand on. The corporate worship, the private worship, the outward expressions of worship that we'll explore in the next chapters all matter deeply, but they only become what they are meant to be when they rise from a heart that has already said, "My whole life is Yours."

Long before Jesus echoed these words, God confronted His people through Isaiah for going through the motions of worship while their hearts were far away from Him, saying they honored Him with their lips but following only human rules they had memorized (Isaiah 29:13). When your everyday choices—how you respond in conflict, how you handle interruption, how you treat the people in front of you—are surrendered to God, your worship is no longer just words or routines. It becomes a whole life offered to Him.

A PRAYER FOR EVERYDAY WORSHIP

Living as a living sacrifice is not about adding more religious activity to your schedule but about inviting God into the ordinary moments that already fill your day. Use this prayer to offer your everyday life back to Him and ask for His help to worship through your choices, conversations, and routines.

God,

Because of Your mercy, I offer my whole life to You today. Take my thoughts, my words, my work, my rest, and my relationships, and make them holy and pleasing to You. Teach me to recognize Your presence in the ordinary moments I usually rush past.

When I am tempted to live on autopilot, renew my mind and remind me that every moment can become worship. Help me choose obedience over comfort, love over irritation, and integrity over convenience, even when no one else sees. Let my ordinary day become a living sacrifice that delights Your heart and points others to You.

Amen.

UNPACKING WORSHIP REALITIES

If it's not big and emotional, it doesn't feel like worship.

Worship is often imagined as big and emotional—lights up, band playing, everyone singing, everyone moved by the Spirit. Those moments are beautiful, but if that is the only way worship is understood, we're missing something vital.

A lifestyle of worship can't be sustained by big, noisy moments alone. It is formed in the quiet, unpolished spaces where no one is leading a song, no one is applauding, and your heart is simply desiring God.

Calmness is not the absence of worship. It is one of the places where worship can finally breathe. Turning off the podcast on your commute, sitting in silence after the kids go to bed, or pausing between meetings to breathe and say, "God, I'm here" may feel small or unproductive, but it is a real act of surrender.

Scripture reminds us that God does not always meet us in dramatic or loud places. When Elijah expected God in the wind, the earthquake, and the fire, the Lord was found instead in a gentle whisper (1 Kings 19:11–12). If worship has mostly meant volume and intensity for you, consider this new invitation: Sometimes worship looks like choosing to be still. You need to be quiet in order to listen.

Through Jesus, therefore, let
us continually offer to God a
sacrifice of praise—the fruit of
lips that openly profess his name.

HEBREWS 13:15

RESONATE: EXPRESSING WORSHIP AND CONNECTING THROUGH PRAISE

The worship we offer on this side of eternity is unlike anything we will ever offer God again. Here on earth, with bodies that ache and hearts that break, we offer praise through struggle and imperfection. This is the only season in our existence where our love for God must push through confusion, disappointment, and loss while we respond to Him with praise.

In every circumstance, we have the choice to worship and draw near to Him. Whether struggling with aging parents or raising children, we learn to turn our eyes to His Word. In the middle of a terminal diagnosis or fresh grief, we decide again and again to put God above everything else.

In heaven, the pain will be gone, the questions will be answered, and worship will flow from perfect joy (Revelation

21:4). But while we're here on earth, our worship carries a different weight. In the midst of the struggle, we choose to magnify God—not with polished performances but with honest affection that chooses Him precisely when it would be easier to turn away.

That kind of devotion doesn't spring from nothing. It grows where attention and obedience are cultivated. A lifestyle of worship is the soil that nourishes every other form of praise. As that lifestyle takes root, two healthy branches grow from it: private worship and corporate worship.

A lifestyle of worship is the ongoing posture of the heart that orients our whole life around pleasing and glorifying God. Our private and corporate worship are the specific, intentional expressions that grow out of that posture—singing, praying, meditating, journaling, listening to worship music, and more.

My goal in this chapter is to help you see what worship can look like. Scripture reveals specific and unique expressions of praise that God delights in, and it gives us language for responses you may already be practicing without realizing it. When you understand the heart behind each expression, it deepens not only your own praise but also your compassion and understanding for the people worshiping around you.

WAYS TO PRAISE

Just as we've done in reshaping how we think about worship, let's now turn our focus to praise. Throughout Scripture, the Hebrew language offers a rich vocabulary for expressing it, yet in English, many of these distinct shades of meaning are compressed into a single word: *praise*.

This matters because each word carries its own posture, tone, and purpose. Praise is not just singing songs. It is a whole vocabulary of movement, sound, and surrendered responses to God.

One way to picture this is by thinking about how we use words in everyday language. We use the word *love* to describe everything from deep covenant commitment to enjoying a favorite meal. The word stays the same, but the meaning shifts with context.

In a similar way, these Hebrew words are like different "accents" in the same language—distinct but complementary ways of expressing the same love for God.

You might consider them different "love languages" of praise. Some expressions you may already practice without having names for them, and others might surprise you or stretch your perspective of what praise looks and sounds like. That's okay. Think of this as an invitation to explore—not a checklist you have to complete.

Halal: Unrestrained, I-Don't-Care-Who's-Watching Joy

Halal is a common root word for praise. Our word *hallelujah* comes from this base word, meaning "to boast in God, to shine, to celebrate Him with such freedom that concern for appearance fades into the background." (For examples, see Psalm 113:1–3 and Nehemiah 12:24.)

Halal is what we glimpse when someone dances, jumps, or sings at full volume because they are more aware of God's goodness than of human opinion. It may stretch you past your comfort zone, but there are moments when love for God wants to look a little undignified.

Yadah: Hands Extended in Surrender

Yadah is praise with outstretched hands. It is worship with extended hands as a physical way of thanking and reaching toward God. Picture the posture of a child reaching up to a parent, the body saying, "I'm Yours, and I want You," even before the mouth says a word. (For examples, see Psalm 63:4 and 2 Chronicles 7:3.)

In seasons of pain, *yadah* can be as simple as lifting your hands when everything in you wants to fold your arms and pull away.

Towdah: Thankful Agreement Before You See It

Towdah also involves extended hands, but with a different motivation. It is thanksgiving offered in advance—praise that says, "I praise You even before the breakthrough," thanking God for things not yet received as well as what is already in hand. (For examples, see Psalm 50:14, 23 and 56:12.)

Towdah is powerful in the middle of uncertainty—a way of honoring God's character and promises when circumstances have not yet changed.

Barak: Kneeling in Reverent Awe

Barak means to kneel or bow in adoration. It is the language of lowered bodies and lifted hearts, quietly acknowledging God's greatness and our smallness. (For examples, see Psalm 95:6 and 1 Chronicles 29:20.)

When life feels heavy, *barak* can look like slipping to your knees beside the bed or bowing your head in the middle of a song, letting your posture express, "You are still King."

Tehillah: The Song That Rises in the Moment

Tehillah is the spontaneous song that flows straight from the heart to God. It is unrehearsed and unpolished—often just a simple phrase sung over and over because that is all you have words for. (For examples, see Psalm 22:3 and Psalm 33:1.)

Tehillah often shows up when written lyrics run out, but your heart keeps talking—humming a line of truth under your breath while folding laundry or singing your own words in the car.

Zamar: Making Music to the Lord

Zamar is praise expressed through music and instruments—plucking strings, playing keys, beating drums. It is what many people first think of when they hear "worship": songs sung with musical accompaniment. (For examples, see Psalm 150 and Psalm 92:1–3.)

Zamar matters because God is worthy of practiced beauty and skill. In seasons of pain, even putting on worship music and letting someone else's *zamar* carry you can be an act of faith.

Shabach: The Shout of Wholehearted Praise

Shabach means "to address in a loud tone, to shout." It is the triumphant cry that rises when you cannot stay silent—praise that sounds like victory even while the battle is still raging. (For examples, see Psalm 63:3–4 and Psalm 117:1.)

Shabach can show up as a shouted "Amen," a loud "Thank You, Jesus," or joining the congregation's shout at the peak of a song. It is praise that refuses to merely whisper God's glory.

None of these expressions is meant to stand alone as the "right" or "more spiritual" way to worship. Problems arise when one expression becomes the whole picture of praise and we start equating real worship with one style or with a certain level of outward intensity instead of the heart behind it.

Think of these seven expressions of worship as seven paths to renewed intimacy with God. Some may feel natural to you, and others may feel unfamiliar or even uncomfortable. But they all lead to the same place. As you keep reading, consider them with an open heart and how you may be able to practice them.

PRIVATE WORSHIP

Early in this book, we talked about the limited view many of us have of worship. When we confine it to Sunday services and events, we miss out on the intimacy and fulfillment God desires for us. If you're taking steps to live a life of worship, the next step is to develop a practice of private worship. Without it, you will eventually feel like something is missing.

Private worship is the overflow of a life of worship. It is what happens when you take specific actions to worship God in the ways He loves. You don't need a leader, you don't need a building or stage, you don't need anyone else watching—just you and God.

This isn't meant to feel like one more thing you have to schedule or cram into your day. When you are living a lifestyle of worship, private worship grows out of that love almost naturally, because when you truly love someone, making space to be with them is not a burden. It becomes an anchor point in your day that helps everything else make sense.

Practically, private worship grows best when you give it a simple, repeatable structure—not to make it a rigid routine but because structure gives your devotion a place to form. Choose a consistent window in your day—a commute, a lunch break, a nap time, or the last ten minutes before bed—and treat it as an appointment with God, not an afterthought.

Bring something to anchor your attention: an open Bible, a short reading plan, or one verse to meditate on. You could also turn on a worship song and practice praising God through one of the seven expressions we explored above.

In private worship, it's simply about you and God. We live in a performance-driven culture where so much of what we do is shaped—consciously or not—by how it will be seen, measured, or perceived by others. It trains us to perform for an audience rather than be present with God. These moments rarely feel impressive, but they are where roots go down—where love for God grows deeper and purer.

Private worship also becomes a beautiful place where costly worship is offered. No one else may ever see you lift your hands in surrender when you get hard news, or hear the cracked voice that sings through tears after another difficult day with a child or a parent. But God sees it all.

Choosing to praise Him in those moments—whether through a shout of praise, a sigh turned into prayer, or an instrument played—is part of the kind of worship you can only give Him on this side of eternity.

Throughout Scripture, we see a consistent pattern: The most visible moments of worship are rooted in unseen devotion. David pours out his heart before the Lord in the quiet places long before leading the people in song (Psalm 63; Psalm 42). Daniel's public faith is sustained by a private rhythm of prayer that no threat could silence (Daniel 6:10). Even Jesus regularly withdrew to solitary places to pray before stepping into public ministry (Mark 1:35).

Without private worship, public worship becomes vulnerable to being just a performance.

Private worship is less about the specific activity and more about the choice to express it because we know that God enjoys it. Whatever shape it takes in a given day, the aim is the same: to turn your full attention toward God, and offer Him a willing, responsive heart.

These private choices train your soul to turn toward God more quickly and more naturally. Your private practice is an extension of the life of worship you are already living—you simply make a conscious choice to *express* your love to God in the ways He has described to us in Scripture.

Then, when you step into corporate worship with others, you are not starting cold. You are bringing a heart and a fire that has already been with the Lord, ready to add your voice to the chorus and shift the atmosphere of the room.

CORPORATE WORSHIP

Corporate worship is what most people think of first when they hear the word *worship*, but as you've seen, it's only part of a much bigger picture.

This might sound like an unusual comparison, but think of corporate worship like playing on a basketball team. A great game doesn't start when the buzzer sounds. For the athlete, it starts long before that.

The player has to live a certain way—eating well, resting, staying conditioned—so their body is ready. That's like a lifestyle of worship, the choices that keep your heart focused on God day after day.

Then there's independent practice. The athlete practices shots alone in the driveway, runs drills, and works on ball-handling when no one is watching. Those unseen reps are like private worship—singing, praying, opening Scripture, turning to God when no one is around. No scoreboard, no crowd, just preparation and follow-through.

And then comes game time. The energy and excitement go up when the player is on the court with the team, running plays together, each person bringing what they've invested in private into a shared moment. That's corporate worship. It's not meant to replace a lifestyle or private practice where those skills are built. It's where everything comes together—where individual devotion becomes a unified expression no person could create alone.

From the outside, corporate worship looks like gathered people, a band or choir, a set list, sound systems, and lyrics on a screen. But at its core, corporate worship is much simpler and profoundly richer than that. It is the people of God together, offering praise to Him in His presence. It is a shared response to who God is and what He has done.

Unfortunately, many approach corporate worship with a consumer mindset, like the service is a concert that exists for their enjoyment. Often, this mindset slips in unnoticed, and it sounds like this: "Worship didn't really do anything for me today" or "They didn't play my song."

Underneath those comments is an assumption that worship is something happening up on the stage that you take in and evaluate, rather than something we participate in as a whole body of worshipers. At its core, this way of thinking doesn't just critique worship; it quietly puts the self at the center of worship.

But learning to lay that mindset down is part of what makes worship so beautiful. The way you approach worship helps set the entire tone for the experience—not only for you but for those around you. When you come to worship expecting to receive a product—something tailored to your preferences and delivered the way you want it—you will almost always walk away disappointed, because that was never the goal of worship.

But when your heart is set on giving God praise and magnifying Him, you will worship regardless of whatever preference is unmet. Worship is about offering, surrendering, and laying down—not receiving,

The personalities, preferences, and postures that interact during corporate worship don't simply shape individuals. Faith, hunger, expectancy, distraction, or unbelief all converge, and the room itself begins to reflect the collective heart. Corporate worship is never neutral. So it is worth asking: Are you drifting toward criticism and passivity, or leaning into faith and participation?

Again, this is why private worship matters. If you have been worshiping God throughout the week, you arrive on Sunday with a prepared heart, and you are not depending on the band to drag you into God's presence. You are prepared with a heart that already says yes, and you join with the yes of others. The room feels different when people come in as participants instead of spectators.

After years of sitting with worship leaders and pastors in coaching rooms and training spaces, I'm convinced of this simple truth: The easiest church to lead in worship is the one that wants to.

Think about the difference it makes for a teacher when a room full of students decide, "We're in. We want to understand this." The same lesson taught to a resistant group feels heavy and hard. Taught to a responsive group, it feels electric.

DIVERSITY IN WORSHIP

As we saw with the ways to praise, there's a lot of diversity, so it's not surprising to see different churches tapping into different expressions of praise. Some traditions are quiet and still with more *barak* than *towdah*—more kneeling and silence than shouting and dancing. Others are loud and expressive, overflowing with *halal* and *shabach*—boisterous celebration and shouted praise.

The outward expression was never meant to be a grading system for someone else's worship or your own. So what can you do if you notice that you're developing a comparison or consumer mindset about worship?

Name it honestly before God. Admit what's going on: "Lord, I'm frustrated because worship isn't meeting my preferences. Help me see this the way You do."

Revisit the ways to praise. Go back to the list and remind yourself of the purpose and heart behind each expression. Before a service, choose one or two expressions to lean into (for example, *yadah* and *towdah*) and set your heart to practice them as an offering, not as a reaction to the set list.

Stretch into the unfamiliar expressions. Consider David's words in 2 Samuel 24:24. When offered an easy shortcut in worship, he refused, saying, "I will not sacrifice to the LORD my God burnt offerings that cost me nothing." Try one form of praise that feels uncomfortable or new and let the discomfort become a small act of humility: "God, my pride feels this, but my heart wants You more than I want my own comfort."

Refocus on who you are there to glorify. Remind yourself: You are not there to manage other people's perceptions of you. You are not performing for the room. You are praising God, and He is not grading your pitch or polish. He delights in sincere praise.

Ask a different question afterward. Instead of "Did I like worship today?" ask, "Did I pursue God today? Did I offer Him anything?" Over time, this new question will slowly retrain your expectations from "What did I get?" to "What did I give?"

Healthy corporate worship comes back to this question: "Who are we here to magnify?"

When we gather, we may sing with raised hands or bowed heads, with quiet tears or loud shouts, with polished music or simple accompaniment. But in every case, the invitation is the same. Bring your whole self, shaped by a lifestyle of worship and rooted in private worship, and join your voice with the voices around you.

Corporate worship is not meant to carry your whole relationship with God. It is meant to echo and amplify it so together we can sing, pray, and respond in ways we could never do it alone.

A PRAYER OF PRAISE AND EXPRESSION

As you consider these different biblical expressions of praise, you may feel both a hunger for more and a little resistance or self-consciousness. Let this prayer help you ask God to free your heart and body to respond to Him with sincere, unhindered worship.

God,

You are worthy of every song, every shout, and every quiet whisper of my heart. Teach me to praise You with freedom, humility, and honesty—not to perform for others but to honor You. Help me bring You my whole self in worship: my voice, my body, my emotions, and my story.

Where fear, self-consciousness, or comparison have held me back, set me free to respond to Your presence with joy. Let my praise draw me closer to You and help others see Your goodness through my life.

Amen.

UNPACKING WORSHIP REALITIES

What do you do when someone else's worship makes you uncomfortable?

Most of us have an internal "worship scale" we use without thinking. One person is too loud, too emotional, too performative. Another is too quiet, too still, too disengaged. We watch hands raised or folded, tears flowing or faces blank, and we assign motives: "They're just trying to get attention," or "They're being fake," or, on the other side, "They clearly don't care," or "Their heart must not be in it."

The problem is that we are trying to read hearts by looking at bodies, and reading hearts is something only God can do.

Scripture gives us a wide, biblically grounded range of praise—*yadah, towdah, barak, tehillah, zamar, halal, shabach*—everything from quiet kneeling to exuberant shouting. Different personalities, church backgrounds, cultures, and seasons of life will naturally lean toward different expressions.

A reserved person may be worshiping deeply with barely a movement. Someone who has just been set free from something may express that freedom with visible passion. Both can be sincere.

Does that mean every visible act is automatically pure and every still moment is holy? Not necessarily. But our job is not to police other people's praise. It's to bring God our own honest response to His constant presence and create a judgment-free space where others can do the same.

One simple way to do this is to turn discomfort into prayer.

Lord,

Thank You for how You are meeting us and for the work You are doing in this congregation's life, even when I cannot see or understand it. Help me lay down judgment and comparison, and teach me to see them the way You do—with grace, mercy, and compassion. Shift my focus from evaluating others to adoring You, and tune my heart to respond to Your presence with humility, joy, and trust.

Amen.

When we lay down the habit of grading each other's praise, we make room for the whole congregation to respond to God with the full, beautiful variety He has already welcomed.

Yet a time is coming and has
now come when the true
worshipers will worship the
Father in the Spirit and in
truth, for they are the kind of
worshipers the Father seeks.

JOHN 4:23

CHAPTER FIVE

REALIGN: WORSHIP'S IMPACT ON LIFE AND COMMUNITY

et me tell you about Terri. She worked for the postal service and sang on the worship team at church, which meant that for a long time she mostly thought about worship in terms of what happened on stage during services. Her job, in her mind, was just her job, and it was a frustrating one because of a coworker who constantly got under her skin and colored the whole atmosphere.

As our worship team began talking about worship as a lifestyle—not just something we do on a stage for an hour on Sunday but something that shapes how we live and respond to everyday moments—something started to shift for her. She sensed the Lord nudging her to do the last thing she wanted to do: pray for that coworker she could not stand, and not in a vague "God please fix them" way, but with genuine care and consideration.

Everything in her resisted. It felt awkward. It felt unfair. But eventually, she chose to obey and prayed sincerely for this coworker. Nothing about Terri's job changed overnight. The coworker did not suddenly become pleasant and easy to deal with. What did change was Terri's heart toward that person and the way she approached the work environment.

Over time, the atmosphere at work began to change for the better. The post office stopped being a place she dreaded and started to look like a field of opportunities where God might actually move—a place where her life of worship and obedience could open doors she could not manufacture on her own.

Terri's story is a modern picture of a true worshiper: someone learning to worship the Father in Spirit and in truth on a Tuesday afternoon, not just on a Sunday stage.

So far, you have explored different expressions of worship, along with the rhythms of private and corporate worship. Now it's time to see what happens when worshiping in Spirit and in truth spills into the places you actually live your life—your home, your workplace, your neighborhood, and your city. What does it feel like when a whole community offers their everyday lives as living sacrifices to God and become the kind of worshipers the Father seeks?

When everyday lives are offered to God, worship no longer stays contained within personal devotion or gathered services. It begins to shape and influence the community you inhabit.

You are becoming a weekday worshiper. You have the chance to treat even the hardest relationships and most overlooked spaces as opportunities to honor God every day. You have the opportunity to trust Him to shape not only your heart but also the relational climate around you in His way and His time. That is what it means to worship in Spirit and in truth when you are off the stage and off the clock.

In John 4, Jesus met a Samaritan woman at a well in the heat of the day—a woman known more for her broken story than for her potential. She was not looking for a spiritual revival. She was just trying to get water at a time when no one would bother her. She didn't know who Jesus was, and she certainly didn't realize that His simple request to give Him a drink was about to disrupt her routine and pull her into a completely different way of seeing God, herself, and her community.

There are three movements in her journey—recognizing, responding, and revival—and each of them shows the transformation that occurs when the revelation of who God is reshapes a life from the inside out. Terri at the post office and the Samaritan woman at the well are separated by centuries, but their stories share the same key moments: an ordinary place, an unexpected encounter with Jesus, a choice to respond, and a ripple effect that impacts others.

Those same moments are available in your story too. They begin when you *recognize* Jesus in the middle of ordinary routines, continue as you *respond*, and mature into a kind of *revival* that cannot be contained. In the pages that follow, this simple progression will serve as a guide for what it means to become a weekday worshiper—one of the true worshipers the Father is seeking—whose life with God impacts far more than a Sunday service.

RECOGNIZING: WHEN JESUS INTERRUPTS "JUST ANOTHER DAY"

For the Samaritan woman, recognizing Jesus did not start with a vision, a song, or a church service. It started with an interruption. She went to the well at a predictable time, in a predictable place, expecting to do what she always did—draw water and get out of the way before anyone could look too closely at her life.

Then Jesus showed up. He asked for a drink, breaking through every social barrier that should have kept them separate—Jew and Samaritan, man and woman, respected leader and scandal-marked outcast. In one simple request, He threw off the script for her day and forced her to look up and pay attention to someone she would normally ignore.

Recognizing Jesus doesn't need to be clouds parting and angels singing. It's the text you did not expect, the conversation you did not plan, the moment in traffic or at the kitchen table when you suddenly sense that "God is doing something here."

Most of the time, weekday worship does not begin with a big emotional swell. It begins with a subtle disruption of your norm, a tug at your intuition, or an invitation to notice Jesus standing in the middle of your regular life and let Him interrupt the way you usually think, feel, and react.

RESPONDING: THE GIFT AND WEIGHT OF "RESPONSE-ABILITY"

Once the Samaritan woman realized this was no ordinary Jewish stranger, she could not go back to pretending she did not know. As they talked, Jesus exposed layers of her story, spoke to the deepest places of her shame, and offered living water she did not even know she needed.

The moment she recognized that Jesus was offering an opportunity to change her life, she had to respond. You could say that she had a "response-ability" to either accept this uncomfortable, revealing conversation with Jesus and let it redefine her worldview or reject it and retreat back into her old patterns.

Before, she could walk to the well in ignorance. Now she had to decide what to do with what she had seen and heard—argue, deflect, walk away, or accept it with an open heart. The same thing happens in your life. There are truths you would almost rather not know, because once you know them, you can no longer shrug and move on.

Spiritually, many of us live with the mentality of "Don't tell me how the hot dogs are made." We sense God putting His finger on an attitude, a habit, a relationship, or a next step, but part of us wants to stay comfortably uninformed because knowledge will force a choice.

Responding in worship means acknowledging "Now that I see You more clearly, I cannot pretend I don't," and allowing that awareness to move you toward trust, repentance, and obedience.

REVIVAL: WHEN A CHANGED LIFE CHANGES A TOWN

When the woman finally reached the point where she could not deny who Jesus was, her response was no secret. She left her water jar, ran back to the very people she had been avoiding, and became the unlikely herald shouting, "Come, see a man who told me everything I ever did!"

Her encounter moved from recognition to response to revival. The transformation in her did not just heal her relationship with God. It sent shockwaves throughout her community as people streamed out to meet Jesus for themselves. Her life became charged with a transformation that affected others. Having tasted and seen God's goodness, she then shared that experience with the people around her.

Many of the Samaritans from that town believed in Jesus because of the woman's testimony (John 4:39). That is what a weekday worshiper is meant to do. A real encounter with Jesus will always expand outward, awakening something in people who have been held down by shame, routine religion, or cultural expectations.

We often think of revival as a huge event and filled stadiums, but often it begins with one person whose worship has been realigned, walking back into familiar streets and relationships with a new story on their lips.

EVERYDAY PRACTICES THAT LOOK LIKE JESUS

Living as a weekday worshiper will rarely look flashy. Most of the time, it looks like recognizing what God is doing and responding with simple acts of love that our culture has stopped paying attention to. It can be as simple as looking up from your phone, making eye contact, and saying good morning to your neighbors on a walk, your coworkers in the hallway, or the kids waiting at the bus stop. Scripture reminds us, "do not forget to do good and to share with others, for with such sacrifices God is pleased" (Hebrews 13:16).

In a world where many people rush past each other without a word, that simple acknowledgment says, "I see you. You matter." That reflects the way Jesus saw people others overlooked.

It can look like smiling at the cashier who seems tired, using their name if they wear a name tag, or being patient when the line moves slowly instead of sighing and making sure everyone knows you are inconvenienced.

It might mean easing back to let a car merge into your lane instead of blocking them, holding the door for the person behind you, or keeping a bottle of water or a snack in your car so you can offer it to someone who is homeless when you stop at a light.

These are more than random, nice gestures. They are intentional choices to put others before you, to show kindness, generosity, forgiveness, and humility—the everyday character of Jesus—without needing a platform or applause.

These simple acts often do more than just brighten someone's day. They build trust, soften defenses, and quietly raise a question in people's minds about the hope and peace they see in you. They draw people to recognize and respond to God.

A simple pattern of showing up with kindness can open surprising doors, like a coworker who finally shares what they are going through, a neighbor who asks you to pray, or a cashier who comments on your thoughtfulness. Suddenly, you find yourself giving words to a story God has already been telling through your life. In that way, everyday worship becomes everyday witness, not because you forced a conversation but because God's love, expressed through you, impacted someone's life.

WORSHIP AS THE FUEL FOR DISCIPLESHIP AND EVANGELISM

Remember when I said that if we get worship right, we get everything else right? If we get worship right, I'm convinced we will get discipleship and evangelism right too.

Discipleship is supposed to mean becoming more like Christ by following Him the way a disciple in Jesus' day followed a rabbi—watching, listening, and imitating until your life starts to look like His.

But instead of that living relationship, many people's "discipleship" is being handed a list of activities: join the Bible study, get in a small group, serve on a team, go on the outreach, and share your faith.

All those are good things to do, but without intimacy with God first, they begin to feel like boxes to check rather than a path to real transformation. It's like trying to turn on a faucet that is not connected to a water line. Twisting the handle harder will not help if you are still disconnected from the water source.

When worship and intimacy with God sit upstream—when your heart is continually turning toward Him in Spirit and in truth—everything else changes. Practices like reading Scripture, praying, fasting, and gathering with others stop being chores you endure to be a "good Christian" and become ways to know and love the God you already desire.

And because many of those practices happen with other people in small groups, teams, or friendships, your worship begins to shape the culture of your community. The way you listen, confess, forgive, and encourage become part of how God disciples others, too, not just you.

Evangelism also feels the effects. Instead of promoting something you have only *heard* should change your life, you find yourself talking about a life that has actually *been changed* and the God who did it. Your witness becomes more natural, like recommending a tool you bought and used in your own home because it actually helped, rather than reciting the marketing description off the package.

This is part of what Jesus meant when He talked about giving us life "to the full" in John 10:10. Seeing each moment as an opportunity for worship is how that fullness expands into parent-teacher conferences, staff meetings, and coffee runs. As worship overflows, your everyday environments become communities where God's love is showcased and others are invited into it.

You can hear the difference in the tone. "I have to go to my Bible study tonight" sounds like an obligation. "I was in

Scripture this morning, and it spoke right into how I handled my kid's meltdown at breakfast. Let me tell you about it." That sounds like overflow.

Everyday stories like how a verse calmed your anxiety before a meeting or how a quiet nudge from God changed the way you treated a team member impact neighbors and friends because they are real and relatable.

This is much closer to how the first disciples lived. They did not invite people to impressive buildings or polished programs. They invited them into a sustaining, worshiping life with Jesus, and entire communities were changed as more people encountered and followed Him.

All this circles back to the question of where the "flow" in your life is coming from. Picture your heart as a vessel and God's presence as oil being poured in—not sticky car oil but fragrant olive oil that brings flavor and healing. When that vessel is being steadily filled through private worship, honest prayer, time in the Word, and gathered worship with others, there is something real to overflow into the rest of your life.

Everyday moments at home, at work, and in your neighborhood become like cups underneath that vessel, catching what spills over as you respond to people and situations with your life of worship. Conversations, decisions, and small acts of kindness carry traces of what God is already doing in you, and your community begins to taste that fullness.

The danger comes when you try to pour without being filled. It is possible to keep doing the activities of discipleship and evangelism—to show up, to serve, to say the right things— while having quietly disconnected from the source that once made those things alive. For a while, the outside can look the same, but inside, the joy and peace begin to dry up.

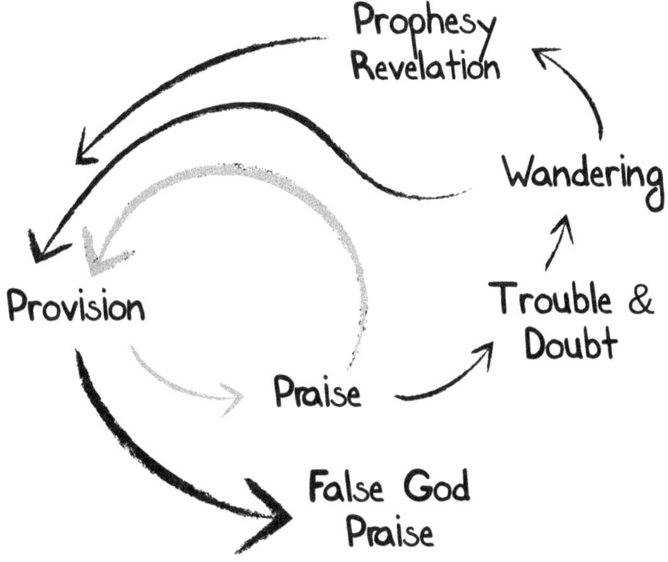

If your cycle of worship is interrupted, the answer is not to push harder at the activity level but to come back to worship and intimacy with God—to let Him fill the vessel again, hearing Jesus' invitation: "Come to me . . . and I will give you rest" (Matthew 11:28). From that place of rest, what He pours into you can once again overflow as life, grace, and strength into the people around you.

LOOKING AHEAD: FROM REALIGNMENT TO DAILY PRACTICE

Terri at the post office and the Samaritan woman at the well showed the same powerful pattern: an everyday moment, an encounter with Jesus, a simple yes, and then ripples of renewal through the people around them.

Recognizing Jesus in the middle of your routines and responding to Him with trust and obedience is how ordinary days become the starting point for community change. This way of life is what some have called *naturally supernatural*—God's power working through very normal moments.

The next step is to make this more than an inspiring idea. The following chapter will guide you into a focused season of practice—a twenty-one-day Reworship Challenge meant to help you live this out one day at a time. You will revisit key truths from earlier chapters, engage with biblical expressions of praise, and take simple, concrete steps in your everyday life so worship does not drift back to Sundays only but becomes the steady rhythm of who you are and how you live.

A PRAYER FOR ALIGNMENT

Worship is meant to touch every part of life, not just the moments that feel "spiritual." Let this prayer help you invite God to realign your priorities, relationships, and daily choices so your whole life becomes worship to Him.

Father,

Realign my heart, my priorities, and my relationships around You. Where my worship has been squeezed into a service or a moment, stretch it into every corner of my life.

Teach me to worship You in the way I work, speak, spend, serve, and love the people around me. Show me any lesser loves that have quietly taken the top place in my heart, and give me grace to lay them down. Make my life a living picture of worship that points my family, my friends, and my community back to You.

Amen.

UNPACKING WORSHIP REALITIES

Do I have to be that weird spiritual person now?

Listen. I get it. You're not the only one to have this thought. If worship is meant to move beyond Sunday into every aspect of life, how do you live that out without becoming the intrusive spiritual person everyone avoids?

Talk about worship in church, and most people nod. Talk about worship at the office, in the grocery store, or in the dugout at your kid's game, and the room can get awkward fast.

There is a real tension between wanting to honor God everywhere and not wanting to force conversations or manufacture spiritual moments that feel fake.

So what does everyday, whole-life worship actually look like on the ground? And how do you tell the difference between Spirit-led boldness and spiritual intrusiveness?

The first part of the answer begins on the inside. Whole-life worship is not a personality type or a constant stream of religious talk. It is an inner posture of availability to God that carries over into ordinary settings.

A weekday worshiper is someone who has already laid their life down in God's presence, so when Tuesday comes, they are simply responding to Him in real time.

The worship reality behind those choices is not spectacle, but surrender and a heart that keeps saying yes to God.

The second part of the answer is about overflow, not overdoing it. A life of worship will sometimes lead to visible moments like encouraging a neighbor, sharing what God has been teaching you, or praying with someone who is open to it—but those moments grow naturally out of genuine intimacy, not pressure to perform.

Intrusiveness shows up when you try to manufacture spiritual encounters on demand or treat every interaction like a sales pitch for faith. Spirit-led boldness, by contrast, is deeply respectful. It listens, notices, and moves only where God is already at work.

When worship is rightly ordered with God at the top, evangelism and discipleship stop being disconnected activities and start to feel like extensions of the life you are already living with God. Time in Scripture, prayer, and gathered worship fills the "reservoir," and your weekday interactions become places where that reservoir can gently spill over.

You are not trying to turn every moment into a mini-church service. You are simply living aware that God is present and willing to let Him realign your reactions, your relationships, and your words.

You do not need to be the loudest spiritual voice in the room when your worship is aligned with God at the top and you approach each day with a heart ready to listen and serve.

Do not merely listen to
the word, and so deceive
yourselves. Do what it says.

JAMES 1:22

CHAPTER SIX

RECOMMIT: A CHALLENGE TO BEGIN YOUR REWORSHIP JOURNEY

n the first five chapters, we've been stretching the way you think about worship. The ideas may feel bigger, clearer, and a little closer to your everyday life than they did before. You may even have found yourself noticing random moments and wondering, "Could this be worship too?"

It's time to take those ideas and new perspectives and put them into practice. Worship doesn't become real in your life just because you read about it. It becomes real when you start arranging your actual days around the God who loves you.

Up to this point, you've walked through some big shifts.

You've seen that you were created to worship—a design that goes all the way back to Eden.

- You've reimagined worship as the orientation of your whole life around what you value most, beyond only expressing it as music.

- You've explored what it means to offer your body as a living sacrifice in ordinary moments.

- You've been introduced to the seven biblical expressions of praise and to private and corporate worship that emerge from a lifestyle, not a playlist.

- You've glimpsed how true worship overflows into discipleship, evangelism, and community when people carry God's presence into their weekday lives.

Now it's time to practice.

This chapter is different from the others on purpose. Instead of more concepts, you'll find a simple, guided practice: the Twenty-One-Day Reworship Challenge. It's not a spiritual boot camp or a test you can fail. It's an invitation to take what you've read and actually live it—one small step, one simple prayer, one ordinary day at a time.

HOW TO USE THIS CHALLENGE

Each day for the next twenty-one days, you'll see three things:

- **Scripture** – a short passage to anchor your heart in God's Word.

Live It Today – one simple, concrete way to respond in real life.

Speak with God – an honest prayer you can make your own.

That's it.

Most days this will take only a few minutes. The goal is consistency over intensity. Some days will stretch you—especially when you try a new expression of praise or step into an unfamiliar act of obedience. Some will feel natural, like you're finally giving language to something your heart has been aware of for a long time. Either way, each day of this challenge will bring you closer to the kind of intimacy with God you were created to experience.

Here are a few guidelines as you begin:

Start where you are, not where you wish you were. This challenge is for everyone. If your worship life feels dry, distracted, or distant, this challenge is for you. If you feel strong and vibrant in worship, this challenge is for you, too, as a way to deepen and sustain what God is already doing. You don't need to be "on fire" to start. You just need to be willing.

Don't wait for perfect conditions. Real life is exactly where worship belongs—car lines, deadlines, walks, and all. If you miss a day, don't quit. Pick up where you left off and keep going.

- **Expect small, quiet shifts more than big fireworks.** God can move dramatically, but often the deepest work happens in small, repeated choices: lifting your hands when you'd rather fold your arms, thanking Him before you see the answer, noticing His presence in the middle of a weekday.

- **Keep something nearby to capture what God shows you.** A simple journal, a notes app on your phone, or even a scrap of paper can help you hold onto what you're noticing and how God is meeting you along the way.

- **Do it with others if you can.** You can walk through these twenty-one days alone, but they often land deeper when you're in community. Consider inviting a friend, your family, your small group, or even your worship team to join you. Share what you're noticing as you go.

THE THREE MOVEMENTS

The challenge is divided into three seven-day movements that mirror the journey of this book.

- **Days 1–7: Reawaken and Realign.** You'll revisit the longing of your heart, the Interrupted Cycle, and your "stack" of priorities—naming lesser loves and placing God back at the top.

Days 8–14: Practice the Seven Expressions. You'll step into the seven Hebrew expressions of praise, in private and corporate settings, learning what each one opens in your heart.

Days 15–21: Live It Out. You'll carry worship into everyday life—relationships, kindness, discipleship, and evangelism—treating your ordinary world as your worship space.

Think of these twenty-one days as spiritual "reps." You're not performing for God. You're training your heart to turn toward Him more quickly and more naturally until worship becomes less of an event and more of a reflex.

A SIMPLE INVITATION

For the next twenty-one days, give God your honest attention. Try the small steps, even when they feel awkward. Pray the simple prayers, even when you don't feel especially spiritual. Watch what happens when you begin to treat every part of your life as a place where worshiping God is possible.

When you're ready, begin with Day 1: You Were Made to Worship.

DAYS 1–7: REAWAKEN AND REALIGN

Day 1 – You Were Made to Worship

- Scripture – Revelation 4:11; Psalm 145 (esp. vv. 1–3)

- Live It Today – Write three to five words or short sentences answering this question: *Why is God worthy of my praise?*

- Speak with God – *"You made me for Yourself; teach me to worship You with my whole life."*

Day 2 – The Interrupted Cycle

- Scripture – Genesis 3:8–10

- Live It Today – Sketch the "Interrupted Cycle of Worship" from Chapter 1 and circle where you feel you are today (trouble, wandering, false gods, return).

- Speak with God – *"Lord, show me where I am and help me return to You again."*

Day 3 – Lesser Loves and Idols

- Scripture – Romans 1:25

- Live It Today – List three to five "lesser loves" that quietly pull your worship away (success, comfort, approval, etc.) and write one sentence each about how they overpromise and underdeliver. Speak with God – *"God, reveal where I've traded You for lesser loves. Help me return my worship to You alone."*

Day 4 – What's at the Top of Your Stack?

Scripture – Matthew 6:33

Live It Today – Draw your "stack" of priorities and honestly place God where He is functionally. Then ask yourself, "Why?"

Speak with God – *"Jesus, move to the top of my stack. Put everything else in its right place beneath You."*

Day 5 – Convenience vs. Costly Worship

Scripture – Genesis 4:3–5

Live It Today – Identify one area where you give God "leftovers," and one costly action you can offer this week (time, attention, generosity, obedience).

Speak with God – *"Lord, I don't want to bring You only what is easy. Show me how to honor You with my first and my best."*

Day 6 – Worship as Life Orientation

Scripture – 1 Corinthians 10:31

Live It Today – Look at your next twenty-four hours and circle three "ordinary" moments (commute, dishes, meeting) where you can consciously say, "This is for You, God."

Speak with God – *"Jesus, You came that I might have life to the full. Teach me to meet You in my ordinary moments today."*

Day 7 – Return and Worship Again

- Scripture – Luke 15:11–24 (Prodigal Son – key verses)

- Live It Today – Write a short "coming home" paragraph, naming where you've wandered and what you're returning from.

- Speak with God – *"Father, I am coming home again. Receive me and restore my worship."*

DAYS 8–14: PRACTICE THE SEVEN EXPRESSIONS

Day 8 – *Yadah* (Hands Extended in Surrender)

- Scripture – Psalm 42:5 (and related *yadah* passages)

- Live It Today – In private, physically lift your hands for at least one song or prayer, saying, "I'm Yours," even if it feels awkward.

- Speak with God – *"God, I stretch out my hands to You. I surrender again and receive Your presence."*

Day 9 – *Towdah* (Thankful Agreement Before You See It)

- Scripture – Psalm 50:23; Psalm 56:12

- Live It Today – Choose one unresolved situation and thank God out loud for His character and promises before anything changes.

Speak with God – *"Lord, I agree with what You have said, even before I see it. I thank You in advance for Your faithfulness."*

Day 10 – *Barak* (Kneeling in Reverent Awe)

Scripture – Psalm 95:6; Psalm 103:1–2

Live It Today – Kneel (or bow your head) for at least two minutes, quietly acknowledging God as King.

Speak with God – *"You are King. I bow before You in awe and trust."*

Day 11 – *Tehillah* (Spontaneous Song)

Scripture – Psalm 22:3; Psalm 33:1

Live It Today – After listening to a song you know, turn the volume down and sing your own simple phrase or line to God, unrehearsed.

Speak with God – *"Lord, receive the song that rises from my heart, even when my words are simple."*

Day 12 – *Zamar* (Making Music to the Lord)

Scripture – Psalm 150; Psalm 92:1–3

Live It Today – Use an instrument or worship playlist and give God ten focused minutes, treating the music itself as your offering.

Speak with God – *"God, thank You for the gift of music. Let every note and every lyric praise You."*

Day 13 – *Halal* (Undignified Joy)

- Scripture – 1 Chronicles 16:4, 10; 2 Samuel 6:14–15 (reference)

- Live It Today – Choose a moment (at home or church) to praise God with more visible joy than usual—sing louder, move, or clap freely.

- Speak with God – *"Lord, free me from fear of what others think. I want to rejoice in You with all my heart."*

Day 14 – *Shabach* (Shout of Praise)

- Scripture – Psalm 117:1; Psalm 63:3–4

- Live It Today – At some point today, give God one wholehearted shout ("Thank You, Jesus!" "You are good!") as an act of faith. Trust me here. Give a real shout of praise from your gut.

- Speak with God – *"God, You are worthy of loud praise! I will not be silent about Your goodness!"*

DAYS 15–21: LIVE IT OUT

Day 15 – Every Moment Is Holy

- Scripture – Romans 12:1–2

- Live It Today – Morning: Pray Romans 12:1 over your life. Evening: Jot down two "ordinary" moments when you sensed God with you.

Speak with God – *"Lord, let my whole life be a living sacrifice today—set apart and pleasing to You."*

Day 16 – Worship in the Everyday (Openness)

Scripture – John 4:7–10

Live It Today – Ask God for one "what if" opportunity today, and then stay open: greet, listen, or encourage one person you'd usually overlook. This doesn't have to be a stranger. It might be someone you know in the grocery store whom you'd rather avoid. Today, don't pretend not to see them.

Speak with God – *"Jesus, open my eyes to the people around me. Use me today to reflect Your heart in one real moment."*

Day 17 – Simple Kindness as Worship

Scripture – Galatians 5:22–23

Live It Today – Do three intentional acts of kindness (be generous, return a shopping cart, say good morning, help at home) and whisper, "This is worship."

Speak with God – *"Holy Spirit, grow Your fruit in me. Let love, joy, peace, patience, kindness, goodness, faithfulness, gentleness, and self-control show up in how I treat people today."*

Day 18 – Overflow, Not Obligation

- Scripture – John 4:28–30

- Live It Today – Share one brief story of God's goodness (not mainly about church or programs) with someone—a friend, text, or social post.

- Speak with God – *"Lord, let my words about You come from real encounter, not obligation. Give me courage to tell what You've done for me."*

Day 19 – Discipleship Fueled by Worship

- Scripture – Psalm 1:1–3

- Live It Today – Spend ten minutes with this passage and first ask, "What does this show me about God?" before "What should I do?"

- Speak with God – *"God, make me like a tree planted by streams of water. Let my delight in You fuel how I grow and change."*

Day 20 – Corporate Worship with a New Posture

- Scripture – Colossians 3:16

- Live It Today – In your next gathered service, notice one lyric or line of Scripture that stands out to you and treat it as God's word to you. Carry it with you through the service and let it gently shape how you sing, listen, and interact with others.

Speak with God – *"Jesus, I come to give, not just to get. Receive my praise today, whatever the songs or setting."*

Day 21 – Reworship Commitment

Scripture – John 4:23–24

Live It Today – Write a short "Worship Rule of Life": three to five simple statements describing how you will keep God at the top of your stack and treat everyday moments as worship going forward.

Speak with God – *"Father, make me a true worshiper who worships in the Spirit and in truth. Keep drawing me back, day after day, into a life of worship."*

AFTER THE TWENTY-ONE DAYS: KEEP GOING

You've just spent twenty-one days deciding to worship, again. You've practiced something you were made for. That is something to celebrate.

You've named longings and lesser loves. You've reordered your stack. You've lifted your hands, knelt, sung new words, shouted praise, and tried to treat ordinary moments as holy. You've stepped into kindness, told stories of God's goodness, and tested what it feels like to carry worship into your weekdays.

Some days probably felt powerful. Others felt ordinary. A few might have felt like nothing was happening at all. That's okay. Real worship is not graded by how dramatic it feels in the moment. It's seen over time in the way your heart keeps turning back toward God.

LOOK BACK WITH GOD

Before you rush back to your schedule and daily life, slow down long enough to look back with God on these twenty-one days. Take a few minutes and sit with questions like these:

- Which day or practice surprised you the most? Why did it stand out?

- Where did you begin to notice your "stack" starting to shift—God moving higher in your real priorities, not just your intentions?

- Did any of the seven expressions of praise feel like a new door into God's presence for you? Which one was it? What happened as you stepped through it?

- How did everyday spaces—work, school, home, errands—feel different when you treated them as places where worship is possible?

- Where did you still feel resistance, distraction, or distance? What might that be revealing about places God is still inviting you to trust Him?

Write a few notes. Talk with a friend or small group if you walked through this together. Someone else will sometimes see growth in you that you would miss on your own.

THE CYCLE CONTINUES

Finishing the challenge does not mean the Interrupted Cycle has disappeared from your life. You will still face trouble, doubt, wandering, and the pull of false gods or lesser loves. The difference now is that you've practiced how to recognize those moments sooner and how to return more quickly.

When you catch yourself drifting—when work climbs to the top of your stack again, when comfort or approval starts to claim your worship, when your worship feels like empty motion—remember what you've already done here.

KEEP YOUR WORSHIP RULE OF LIFE ALIVE

On Day 21, you wrote a simple Worship Rule of Life—three to five statements describing how you want to keep God at the top and treat everyday moments as worship. Don't let that just sit on the page.

Consider this:

> Posting it where you'll see it. On your bathroom mirror, your fridge, your desk, or your phone's lock screen.

> Revisiting and adjusting it. Every few months, read it with God. What still fits your current season? What needs to be sharpened, simplified, or added?

> Sharing it with someone. Let at least one trusted friend or group know what you're aiming for. Invite them to ask you how it's going.

Your Rule of Life is not a list of rules to earn God's favor. It's a way of protecting the space in your heart that only God is meant to fill.

DON'T WALK THIS ALONE

Worship is deeply personal, but it was never meant to stay private.

Imagine a church where dozens or hundreds of people have walked a journey like the one you just finished. People who come into corporate worship as participants, not spectators. People who carry the presence of God into weekday offices, classrooms, and neighborhoods. People who, like the Samaritan woman, can't help but say, "Come, see the One who has met me where I am."

If this challenge has stirred something in you, consider:

- Repeating it with a friend, spouse, or small group.

- Sharing it with your worship team or pastor as a way to deepen the heart behind your church's worship, not just its set lists.

- Adapting pieces of it for your kids or students, using simpler language but the same heartbeat.

You don't have to start a program. Just invite a few others to practice worship as a lifestyle alongside you.

A PRAYER FOR THE JOURNEY AHEAD

Father,

Thank You for every moment of worship You've drawn out of my heart throughout this challenge. Forgive me for the lesser loves that still compete for my attention and affection.

Keep showing me when my stack is out of order, and lead me back to putting You first.

Teach me to live as a living sacrifice wherever I am, and let my worship overflow into kindness, courage, and love for the people around me.

Make me a true worshiper who worships in the Spirit and in truth. And when I wander, remind me that the invitation is always the same: to return, to worship again, and to find my life in You.

Amen.

WHEN RECOGNITION CHANGES YOU

We've come a long way together. We began in the Garden of Eden where worship was not learned or scheduled—it was the joyful response of enjoying God's presence and provision, simply living life with Him. From there, Adam and Eve chose not to worship, and we discovered the interruption we still live with today—the way worship drifts, fractures, and gets misplaced.

We stepped back and looked at worship from different angles—how it is lost and rediscovered, how it is corrected and renewed, and how moments under leaders like Josiah and Ezra reveal what happens when hearts are reordered around God. Throughout it all, one truth has remained steady: Worship has always been about posture, not location.

We explored that posture in gathered moments and in private ones, in public expressions and unseen decisions, following worship from the "top of the stack" in your priorities all the way down into the way you speak, drive, work, and love.

Now you know that worship is not just something you do. It is the purpose for which you were created, the orientation of your entire life around the One who is worthy of it all. That ache you sometimes feel—that sense that something is missing even when life is full—is the longing for the surrender and intimacy with God you were made for. And as you have seen throughout these pages, when worship is in its right place—God above everything else—the other elements of your life can move into their right places and take on their true power and meaning (Acts 17:27–28).

You can no longer deny that God's presence and provision have been there all along, always waiting with open arms for you to come back. Like the woman at the well who recognized Jesus, you cannot "unknow" that worship is your purpose. You cannot honestly say you never knew there was more to worship than a music set or a Sunday routine. You are standing at a crossroads that will not just change how you sing, but how you live.

The question is this: *What choice will you make?*

You can choose to continue as you were before you read this book, cramming worship into Sunday mornings, weekend retreats, and occasional "spiritual highs." Or you can choose to set your heart and your mind toward God every day and strive to live a life of worship.

This will be an imperfect effort, trust me. I've been pursuing the Lord this way for the past twenty years. You will not suddenly become a flawless worshiper who always feels close to God. You may forget, get distracted, and fall back into old rhythms.

But here's the hope woven through the entire story, and that hope is that there has always been an invitation back. As I shared in Chapter 1, Jesus stepped into the interruption we could not fix. He paid the price of death and rose again so we could be restored—not just forgiven, but brought back into the fullness of relationship with God.

If you have put your faith in Jesus Christ, this is where everything changes. What once felt like pressure or performance no longer defines your worship. Spiritual checklists may have kept you busy, striving, or distracted, but it no longer gets to set the rhythm of your life. You are free to worship God again—not earnestly, not anxiously, but freely, responding to His presence and provision the way you were always meant to.

Whatever your past has looked like, today is a new chance to decide. Choose a life of worship—one ordinary, surrendered moment at a time—and let God reorder everything else from there. Don't ignore the stirring of your heart.

WHEN REAL LIFE TESTS YOU

New understanding often brings new desire and energy. You may feel a renewed drive to live a lifestyle of worship, to put God at the top of your stack, to offer your life as a living sacrifice, and to let your days be marked by intimacy rather than distance. Don't rush past or resist that desire. That is the Holy Spirit nudging you to keep going.

This new journey will be rewarding, but it will also challenge you in some unexpected ways. Adjusting your life to worship takes effort and practice. It may not feel hard today or maybe even this week while the ideas are fresh. It might feel hard in two weeks when your calendar fills up again, your phone pulls you back in, and the usual patterns unconsciously slide back into place.

It may feel hard on an ordinary weekday when you are packing lunches, answering emails, or sitting in traffic, when nothing around you feels "spiritual" and you feel numb or distracted.

But the biggest challenge you will face may be when the evidence of your transformation is not obvious on the outside. Much of the work of living a life of worship will happen in places no one else will ever see—in your private time, in the thoughts you surrender, in the choices you make when no one is watching, in the quiet "yes" to God that never becomes a social media moment.

In a culture that craves outside validation, it can be difficult to do something that is between you and God. Consider simple ways to anchor your heart, like journaling personal wins no one else sees, sharing with a trusted friend who will pray for you, or setting reminders that prompt you to pause and remember who you are really living for.

Eventually, your inner life of worship will spill out into the way you move throughout the world, but most people will never know all the dedication and intention you have put in. What they will notice is that you are slower to take offense, quicker to forgive, more patient, more present in conversations, and more grounded when circumstances are shaky. They will see a steadier peace, a quieter confidence, and a different approach to disappointment and success.

Scripture calls this fruit—love, joy, peace, patience, kindness, goodness, faithfulness, gentleness, and self-control. It's not something you manufacture through effort but something the Spirit grows in you as your life stays rooted in God's presence.

A SIMPLE PATTERN FOR A BUSY LIFE

Because the work of choosing to worship is ongoing, you will need more than a burst of inspiration. You will need consistency through a simple pattern that you do not have to reinvent every day. That is one of the reasons Romans 12 has been a central anchor in this book. It gives you a clear picture of what it means to live as a "living sacrifice"—not a one-time moment, but a posture that can shape your days.

When your efforts fail or your motivation wanes, come back to this pattern discussed in Chapter 3:

- **Morning:** Offer your day. Present your body, your schedule, your energy, and your relationships to God as an act of worship, acknowledging that your life belongs to Him.

- **Midday:** Renew your mind. Pause long enough to let God's truth interrupt hurry, stress, and distraction so you are not "conformed to the pattern of this world" without realizing it.

- **Evening:** Reflect with God. Look back on your day honestly, with gratitude for where you walked as a living sacrifice and openness about where you drifted, letting God's voice interpret your story.

This will not remove every struggle, but it is a way of saying, over and over, "God, I want You at the highest place in my life, not just in theory but in how I actually live." Over time, it trains your instincts so worship is not something you visit occasionally but the way you move throughout your life.

Take comfort in knowing that you were not meant to do this perfectly. You are an imperfect human navigating the imperfect cycle of worship, so when you misstep or get distracted, don't waste time beating yourself up about it. God doesn't want that. Just as He searched for Adam and Eve in the Garden of Eden when they were hiding in shame, He just wants you back. And each time you return to Him, the Interrupted Cycle becomes, once more, a story of renewed intimacy.

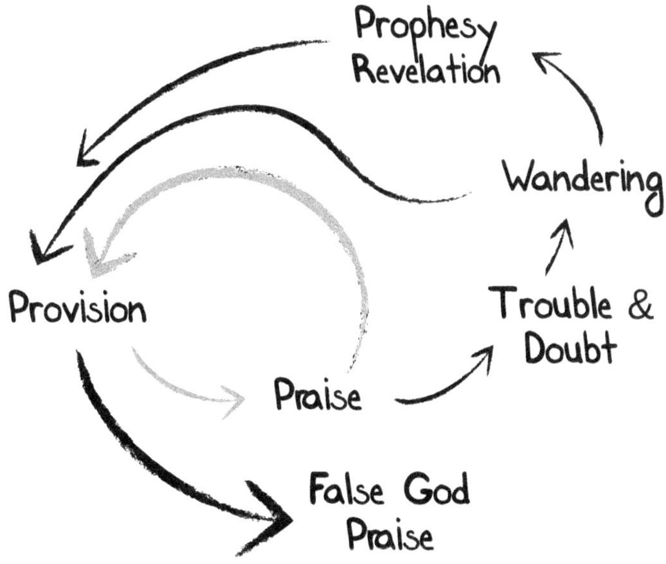

YOU INFLUENCE MORE THAN YOU KNOW

When your life is reordered around God, the people around you will experience the difference, even if they cannot put words to it yet. They may first notice a different kind of peace in you, a different patience, a different way you move through conflict, waiting, or celebration. They may not know that what they are seeing is the life of a worshiper, but they will feel its effects.

Jesus came so you could escape emptiness and live the "abundant life" He promised, marked by joy, meaning, and resilience that spills over into every relationship and setting.

As that happens, you may find yourself wanting others to taste what you are beginning to experience. Maybe a friend who is restless in church comes to mind, or a family member who feels numb during worship, or someone in your small group who knows there must be more. If this book has helped you see worship differently, let that spill over naturally by telling your story, asking honest questions about what sits at the top of their stacks, or even by putting this book in their hands and walking through it side by side.

Your life of worship can become an invitation for someone else. As you live surrendered in your ordinary spaces, you are not just "doing better spiritually." Your surrendered life becomes one of the powerful ways God draws others back into the life of worship they were created for.

A CLOSING PRAYER FROM THE CHURCH BEFORE US

As we close this book, I want to end not with my own words but with a prayer that has shaped the worship life of the church across generations. *The Book of Common Prayer*, first compiled in 1549, brought Scripture and historic prayers together to give God's people shared words that shape their hearts, not just outline their services.

Throughout these pages, I've purposely quoted voices from different Christian traditions. True worship humbles us, helps us receive from others, and reminds us that the church is bigger than our own preferences. I want to close with a prayer from *The Book of Common Prayer* that names what many of us know well—distraction, drift, and divided attention—and simply ask God to meet us there. May your life be marked and blessed by the daily choice to reworship.

A PRAYER FOR WORSHIP

Book of Common Prayer (1979), Other Prayers #64

O Almighty God,
who pourest out on all who desire it
the spirit of grace and of supplication:
Deliver us, when we draw near to thee,
from coldness of heart and wanderings of mind,
that with steadfast thoughts and kindled affections
we may worship thee in spirit and in truth;
through Jesus Christ our Lord.

Amen.

OLD TESTAMENT EXPRESSIONS OF WORSHIP

orship didn't begin with a service, a structure, or a song. Long before there was a temple, a priesthood, or an organized gathering, people responded to God through obedience, sacrifice, prayer, and remembrance.

As you move through Scripture, you'll see worship take on more defined forms. Through Moses, God establishes a pattern for worship ordered around sacrifice, priesthood, and sacred space. Later, with David, we see further development—especially in the structure and expression of musical praise—built alongside what God had already established.

What I'm sharing here isn't an exhaustive list—but it is a way to see how worship has been expressed across Scripture over thousands of years, and to recognize that what we often think of as "worship" today is only part of a much bigger story.

A. EXPRESSIONS OF WORSHIP

Expression	Scripture	Description
Sacrifice / offering	Genesis 4:3–5; Genesis 8:20; Leviticus 1–7	Expression of devotion, thanksgiving, repentance, and atonement
Obedience	1 Samuel 15:22; Genesis 22	"To obey is better than sacrifice" — worship begins with saying yes to God
Altar building, remembrance, memorial stones	Genesis 12:6, 8 & 18; Genesis 35:7 ; Exodus 17:15	Physical memorials that mark God's presence and faithfulness
Blessing / dedication	Numbers 6:24–26	Declaring God's character and favor over His people
Bowing / prostration	Genesis 24:26; Exodus 4:31; Exodus 34:8	Posture of humility, surrender, and reverence
Shouting / Trumpets	Numbers 10; Joshua 6	Victory proclamation and faith declaration. Festival worship.
Dancing / Tambourines	Exodus 15:20; Judges 21:21; Judges 11:34	Joyful, praise, celebration

B. FORMATIONS OF ORDERED WORSHIP

Mosaic Worship (Tabernacle)

As God forms a people for Himself, worship becomes structured.

Exodus 25–31 — Instructions for the tabernacle

Exodus 35–40 — The tabernacle is built and filled with God's presence

Leviticus 1–7 — Sacrificial system

Leviticus 16 — Day of Atonement

Numbers 28–29 — Appointed offerings and rhythms

This is where worship becomes ordered—centered on sacrifice, priesthood, and the presence of God dwelling among His people.

Davidic Worship (Temple-Era Expression)

Later, under David, worship expands in expression—especially through music. Much of what we are familiar with in worship today is shaped by the life and songs of David, who, while not a perfect model, gives us one of the clearest biblical pictures of a life oriented toward God in worship.

1 Chronicles 15–16 — The ark is brought to Jerusalem with singing and instruments

1 Chronicles 23–25 — Musicians are appointed for continual praise

- **2 Chronicles 5–7** — Temple worship established (under Solomon)

David organizes musical worship and integrates it into the life of the people. While the temple itself is built under Solomon, what we often recognize as "musical worship" is deeply shaped by what David established.

C. OLD TESTAMENT MUSICAL EXPRESSIONS OF WORSHIP

Throughout the Old Testament, there are many songs that appear outside of what most people are familiar with in the Psalms and other poetic books in the bible. Here are a few:

- **Song of Moses** — Exodus 15
- **Miriam's song, dancing, and tambourine** — Exodus 15:20–21
- **Song of Deborah** — Judges 5
- **Hannah's Praise** — 1 Samuel 2

These remind us that musical worship didn't begin with the Psalms—it has always been part of how people respond to God.

Why This Matters

For many of us, our understanding of worship has been shaped by a relatively small window of church history—often just the last few decades.

But as you can see Scripture tells a much bigger story.

When you begin to see how worship has been expressed across thousands of years it expands your understanding and shows us how we can worship.

Worship isn't confined to a moment.

It has always shaped the lives of God's people.

TIMELINE OF WORSHIP

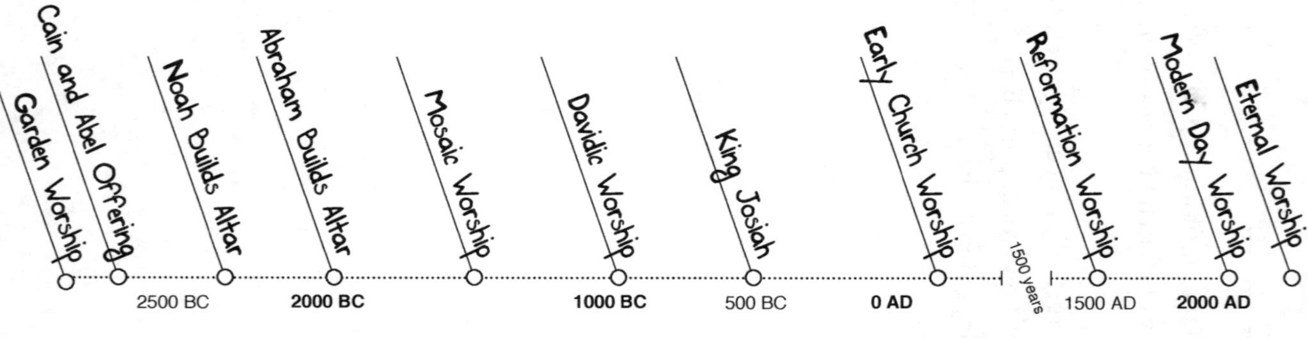

To learn more: Scan the QR code or visit reworship.___/timeline.

BIBLICAL EXPRESSIONS OF PRAISE IN TODAY'S CHURCH

his appendix is a simple reference to help you connect the biblical Hebrew words for praise with Scripture and some of the worship songs many churches sing today. It isn't a list of "approved" songs, just examples based on the CCLI Top 100 that carry the same heart and expression.

1. *HALLAL*

Meaning: To praise, boast, celebrate, shine; joyful, visible, exuberant praise (root of "Hallelujah").
Scripture: Psalm 113:1–3; Psalm 149:3; Psalm 150:1–6
Song examples:

- "Praise" — Brandon Lake, Chandler Moore, Chris Brown, Cody Carnes, Pat Barrett, Steven Furtick

- "Raise a Hallelujah" — Jake Stevens, Jonathan David Helser, Melissa Helser, Molly Skaggs

- "House of the Lord" — Jonathan Smith, Phil Wickham

- "Great Things" — Jonas Myrin, Phil Wickham

2. *YADAH*

Meaning: To extend the hands; thanksgiving expressed outwardly.
Scripture: Psalm 63:4; Psalm 107:15; 2 Chronicles 20:21
Song examples:

- "10,000 Reasons (Bless the Lord)" — Jonas Myrin, Matt Redman

- "Goodness of God" — Ben Fielding, Brian Johnson, Ed Cash, Jason Ingram, Jenn Johnson

- "Gratitude" — Benjamin Hastings, Brandon Lake, Dante Bowe

- "God, I'm Just Grateful" — Abubakar Baker Shariff-Farr, Chandler Moore, Joshua Emanuel Coleman, Pat Barrett, Steven Furtick

3. *TOWDAH*

Meaning: Thanksgiving offered in faith—often before the outcome is seen.
Scripture: Psalm 50:14; Psalm 50:23; Psalm 56:12
Song examples:

- "It Is Well with My Soul" — Horatio Gates Spafford, Philip Paul Bliss

- "Trust in God" — Brandon Lake, Chris Brown, Mitch Wong, Steven Furtick

- "Living Hope" — Brian Johnson, Phil Wickham

"Firm Foundation (He Won't)" — Austin Davis, Chandler Moore, Cody Carnes

4. *SHABACH*

Meaning: To shout, proclaim, or declare triumph.
Scripture: Psalm 47:1; Psalm 145:4; Isaiah 12:6
Song examples:

"Shout to the Lord" — Darlene Zschech

"This Is Amazing Grace" — Jeremy Riddle, Josh Farro, Phil Wickham

"Glorious Day" — Jason Ingram, Jonathan Smith, Kristian Stanfill, Sean Curran

"I Thank God" — Aaron Moses, Chuck Butler, Dante Bowe, Enrique Holmes, Jesse Cline, Maryanne J. George

5. *BARAK*

Meaning: To kneel, bow low, bless God in reverence and surrender.
Scripture: Psalm 95:6; Psalm 34:1; 1 Chronicles 29:20
Song examples:

"Here I Am to Worship" — Tim Hughes

"I Surrender All" — Judson Wheeler Van DeVenter, Winfield Scott Weeden

"We Fall Down" — Chris Tomlin

"Nothing Else" — Cody Carnes, Hank Bentley, Jessie Early

6. *ZAMAR*

Meaning: To sing and make music; praise with instruments and skill.
Scripture: Psalm 21:13; Psalm 57:8–9; 1 Chronicles 16:9; Psalm 150
Song examples:

- "Great Are You, Lord" — David Leonard, Jason Ingram, Leslie Jordan

- "O Praise the Name (Anástasis)" — Benjamin Hastings, Dean Ussher, Marty Sampson

- "What an Awesome God" — Jonathan Smith, Phil Wickham, Rich Mullins

- "All Glory Be to Christ" — Dustin Kensrue

7. *TEHILLAH*

Meaning: Spirit-led, sung praise; the song itself as an offering.
Scripture: Psalm 22:3; Isaiah 61:3; Deuteronomy 10:21
Song examples:

- "Holy Forever" — Brian Johnson, Chris Tomlin, Jason Ingram, Jenn Johnson, Phil Wickham

- "Holy Holy Holy (Nicaea)" — Reginald Heber, John Bacchus Dykes

- "The Heart of Worship" — Matt Redman

- "Revelation Song" — Jennie Lee Riddle

REWORSHIP IS MORE THAN A BOOK

Reworship is a movement. It's an invitation into a different way of living with God.

This book is just the beginning of the worship journey that God has in store for you. When worship is rightly placed, joy, clarity, and purpose begin to flow from it. Reworship exists to help you return to true worship—not just services or songs but real intimacy with God. As you keep walking this out, you'll grow in:

Restored intimacy: Returning to God, not out of religion, but relationship.

Personal renewal: Deepening your character and spiritual life so you live from overflow, not obligation.

Ministry foundations: Strengthening teams and culture so your life and community become healthy and thriving.

Multiplying worshipers: Investing in others so more people experience a lifestyle of worship.

If something stirred in you while reading this book, don't let it stop here. Scan the QR code or visit reworship.com/book to:

- Explore tools for living a life of true worship in your everyday rhythms.

- Find resources and trainings you can use personally or with your team, small group, or church.

- Stay connected for new content, updates, and future ways to engage with this movement.

Mike Seay is a worshipper, husband, and dad of three who has spent more than twenty years helping people encounter God through leading worship and creative ministry. He is the cofounder of Multiply Group, which equips churches to intentionally multiply healthy leaders, and the founder of ReWorship—a movement equipping believers, worship leaders, and churches to rediscover the heart of worship and cultivate thriving worship communities.

www.ingramcontent.com/pod-product-compliance
Lightning Source LLC
Chambersburg PA
CBHW052014150726
47999CB00004B/1650